ABORIGINAL AMERICA

(American History, Vol. I)

ABORIGINAL AMERICA

(American History, Vol. I)

JACOB ABBOTT

WILDSIDE PRESS

Aboriginal America (American History, Vol. I)

Originally published in 1860.

Published in 2009 by Wildside Press.
www.wildsidepress.com

CONTENTS

Preface 7

Types of Life in America 9

Face of the Country 24

Remarkable Plants 37

Remarkable Animals 47

The Indian Races 63

The Indian Family 75

Mechanic Arts 89

Indian Legends and Tales 105

Constitution and Character of the Indian Mind 121

The Coming of the Europeans 131

PREFACE

It is the design of this work to narrate, in a clear, simple, and intelligible manner, the leading events connected with the history of our country, from the earliest periods, down, as nearly as practicable, to the present time. The work is intended to comprise, in a distinct and connected narrative, all that it is essential for the general reader to understand in respect to the subject of it, while for those who have time for more extended studies, it may serve as an introduction to other and more copious sources of information.

The author hopes also that the work may be found useful to the young, in awakening in their minds an interest in the history of their country, and a desire for further instruction in respect to it. While it is doubtless true that such a subject can be really grasped only by minds in some degree mature, still the author believes that many young persons, especially such as are intelligent and thoughtful in disposition and character, may derive both entertainment and instruction from a perusal of these pages.

TYPES OF LIFE IN AMERICA

Subject of the Volume

The first step to be taken in studying the history of our country is to form some clear and proper conception of the characteristics and condition of the territory which is now occupied by the American people, as it existed when first discovered and explored by Europeans. The aboriginal condition of the country, therefore, anterior to its occupation by white men, and the character and condition of the native tribes which then inhabited it, will be the subject of this volume.

Origin of Vegetable and Animal Life in America

When the new world was first discovered it was found to be, like the old, well stocked with plants and animals, and inhabited by a great many tribes and nations of men; and yet the plants and animals, if not the men, were all essentially different from those known in the old world. This was unexpected; it was thought to be quite remarkable, and it added greatly to the difficulty of deciding the question, which, of course, at once arose, in respect to the origin of these plants and animals and men, and to the manner in which they came in possession of a continent thus cut off apparently from all intercourse and connection with the rest of the world.

For the American continent is entirely separated from the old. The nearest approach which it makes to it in any part is at Behring's Straits, on the north-west, where it is divided form the Asiatic continent by a channel about forty miles wide.

Means of Communication With the Old World.

Some animals and perhaps some plants, and most certainly man, may be supposed to have been transported across such a channel of water as this of Behring's Straits, either by boats made by the savages living on the coasts, or possibly by means of ice, either upon moving fields driven by the wind, or upon the solid surface, at some time when the whole channel was entirely frozen over.

There is also at some distance south of Behring's Straits a remarkable chain of islands, called the Aleutian Islands, which extend in a regular and continuous line from the American to the Asiatic shore. These islands are nearly all inhabited, and the natives navigate the seas around them in boats made of a frame-work of wood or bone, covered externally with seal skins.

These islands are volcanic. They contain now numerous volcanoes, some active and some extinct, and also hot springs and other indications of subterranean fire. They bear no trees, but they produce a great variety of animals. They look, upon the map, like a row of stepping stones, placed on purpose to enable men and animals from the old world to make their way to the new.

It is perhaps possible to imagine also that a company of men might have been forced accidentally to sea in some large canoe from the coast of Africa, or on the other side from some of the islands of the Pacific, and so driven across the intervening water, and landed upon the American shores. It is true that it would be exceedingly improbable that any such combination of circumstances would occur as could lead to such a result. The canoe or boat must have been very large, the stock of provisions very great, and the wind, while it must not have been violent enough to engulf the boat, must still have blown very long. and very steadily to have carried a company of men so far before they all perished of hunger and thirst. All this would have been very improbable. Still it would be difficult to show that it could not occur. From the hundreds and perhaps thousands of boats full of savages that have been blown off to sea from the coasts of Africa, or from the South Sea Islands, it would be impossible to prove positively that there could never have been one that by any chance could have reached the American shores.

There is still another mode by which we can imagine the animal and vegetable life of America to have been communicated to it from other regions, and that is, by supposing that there was in former ages some direct connection between the two continents by a tract of land which has since become submerged. It is well known now that the crust of the earth is not in a stable condition. It is subject to changes and movements of various kinds, which are now going forward all the time, and have probably always been going forward. In some places the land is slowly rising; in others it is slowly subsiding. There are many places in the world where towns and cities which formerly stood high and dry on the land are now under water. The land has slowly subsided, so that the sea at the present time flows over it, and people passing in boats now look down and see the old foundations, and fragments of the fallen walls and columns, at the bottom.

The rising and sinking of the land in this way can only be directly and positively proved in places which lie along the sea shore, for nowhere else is there any exact standard of comparison by which the rising or falling may be measured. But it is now generally believed by geologists and philosophers that a state of gradual motion, rising in some places and sinking in others, is the natural and constant condition, or, as it is more scientifically expressed, the normal condition of the strata which form the crust of the globe. Of the causes which lead to this state of things it would be out of place to speak here, but there is no doubt of the fact; and this action is in no part of the world going on so actively and with so sensible an effect as on some of the coasts of America.

Now, although these changes of level proceed in an extremely gradual manner, so that the inhabitants that dwell upon the territory thus slowly rising or falling are, in most cases, wholly unconscious of the motion, still the effect might be sufficient, in the course of forty or fifty centuries, to submerge a very extensive tract of land, which in remote ages may have formed a connection between the American continent and other lands lying to the eastward or westward of it.

The Plants and Animals of America Generally New.

These and various other similar theories were devised in former times in endeavors to contrive some way of bringing plants and animals from other countries to America; but they have been generally considered unsatisfactory, since on coming fully to examine the plants and animals living here, they were found to be, as it seemed, essentially different from those found in other countries, so different as to render it very improbable, according to the ideas on this subject that have hitherto generally prevailed, that they could ever be descended from the same stock, at least by ordinary generation. The fauna and the flora were both found to be in general essentially dissimilar.

We say in general, for there are some animals, such as birds, that might easily fly across the ocean, and sea-weeds, that might drift across, and polar animals, such as bears, seals, foxes and dogs, and the like, which go and come as they will, all over the Arctic seas, that were found common to both worlds. With a moderate number of exceptions such as these, however, the plants and animals found in America proved on examination to be entirely new.

By the fauna of a country is meant the system of animals that inhabit it. The flora is its system of plants. Now, inasmuch as both the fauna and the flora of America were so essentially different from those of the old world, that, so far as could be judged from all that was known of the propagation of plants and animals, and of the changes which they may undergo from the influence of climate and soil, and other conditions, the one system, in the opinion of naturalists, could not have been produced from the other, it seemed to be wholly useless to attempt to contrive means by which the progenitors of the present races in America could have been wafted across the ocean, or could have migrated by means of countries and territories which once existed, but are now submerged.

Man Admitted to be an Exception

This reasoning, however, applied only to plants and to inferior animals, but not to man; for the races of men found upon this continent were deemed by naturalists to be of the same species with all the other races now existing in the world: that is, too difference between the different races of men were judged to be not specific differences, that is, not such as to preclude the possibility of their all being deduced from one original pair. This has always been the general opinion among naturalists, and in their systems of classification all the various races of men are classed as one species. Man, therefore, it has always been admitted, may have been brought to America over the ice at Behring's Straits, or by boats blown off from the coast of Africa, or from the islands in the Pacific; but the general stocking of the country with its countless thousands of species, both of animals and vegetable life, it was thought could not be thus explained.

What is a Species?

The degree of probability that the present plants and animals of America could not have been derived, within a modern period, and by direct descent, from those of the old world, depends, of course, upon the degree of difference there is between them, because there is a certain degree of difference, and that not small, which changes of climate and soil, and of other conditions of that kind will account for; but the difference in question was found to be very great indeed. It is a specific difference, that is, a difference in the species .

A species of plants or animals, as the term has been generally used by naturalists, comprises all such individuals as are so similar to each other that we may suppose them all to have proceeded from one common parentage, and so dissimilar from all others that they could not have been reproduced from the others, nor the others produced from them, by ordinary generation.

Whether there be or not some extraordinary mode by which at rare and distant intervals, and under conditions seldom occurring, and which have not occurred under the observation of men, by which anew species can arise, having its origin, in some way or other, in a former species, in the same sense as now a new individual, of the same species, has it origin in a former individual of the same species, by the production of a seed or an egg, for example; or whether it may not be possible that in an exceedingly great length of time, and by means of a very long-continued accumulation of minute and almost imperceptible changes, one species should be transformed into another, or, by branching, give origin to several others, adapted to new and peculiar circumstances arising in the world's history, are questions which are now greatly agitated among the learned, and may not soon be settled. All we know is, that the plants and animals throughout the world exist in species, each one of which stands at present distinct and isolated wholly apart from all the rest, and one cannot be transformed into another by ordinary generation, through changes of soil and climate, or any other causes whatever known to man, within so short a period as six thousand years.

The apple, for instance, is one species, and the pear is another. In many respects they are similar to each other, and each may be changed by cultivation and by the operation of other causes a great deal, but by no possibility can one be derived from the other. By different modes of cultivation, by different selections of seeds, by changes in soil, and by other such means, a horticulturist may vary the character of his apples very much. He may produce large apples and small apples, sweet apples and sour apples, apples with a skin red, green, yellow, or brown, but he can never produce a pear. The apple, under all it modifications, will remain an apple still. It is a species by itself, separated from all other species whatever by a fixed and permanent bound, which it is impossible, as has always been supposed, that it can ever pass.

It is the same with animals. Each one is subject to a great many modifications in respect to its form, its size, its color, and even it faculties, but through all these changes each on remains entirely within its own bounds, as it were. The distinguishing characteristics of the species remain distinguishing characteristics of the species remain unchanged. Take for instance, any species of the dog. We may, perhaps, by means of differences of treatment, of food, of climate, or of immediate parentage, procure big dogs and little dogs, weak dogs and strong dogs, gentle dogs and fierce dogs, all proceeding from the same original stock, but we can have no cats, nor anything that shall bear the least specific resemblance to a cat.

The Distinction of Species Very Permanent

It may, perhaps, be said that although in the comparatively short periods of time that have been covered by the experiments and observations which have been made by man, the transformation of one species into another may have been impossible, still such changes may have been effected in longer periods, and that the various forms of animal and vegetable life which now exist upon the earth may have proceeded from some common origin, or at least from some moderate number of original types existing in former ages. And, indeed, this may possibly be so. But there seems to be quite satisfactory evidence to prove that the distinction of species is as permanent in respect to the past and the future, at least for very long periods, as it is decisive at the present time.

Evidence of Ancient Records

In the first place, we have in Egyptian and Assyrian monuments, which go back with their records several thousand years — much more than half the time, according to the usually received opinion, since the earth was stocked with the present races of animals — many drawings and other representations of plants and animals as they existed then, and even seeds, in some cases, found in the wrappings of Egyptian mummies, all of which show that these plants and animals, and even the races of men, were specifically the same then as now. There have been no changes whatever that encroach at all upon the limits and bounds by which the different species are separated from each other at the present day, or confuse the lines of demarcation in any degree. There is no approach of one type toward another, nor any tendency to such an approach. Now, is a change could be effected in the specific character of a plant or of an animal, in any limited series of generations, we should be very likely to find evidences of it in a period of three or four thousand years, especially in the case of such animals as arrive at maturity in a short time, and thus in any given period reckon as many generations as years. Between the bird carved upon an Egyptian or Assyrian slab, and its representative at the present day, probably three thousand generations may have intervened, and yet the present living specimen is specifically identical with the delineation of its ancestor. The great comparative anatomist Cuvier examined the mummy of an ibis, from three to four thousand years old, comparing it minutely with a living bird of the present day, and found the two specimens in all respects identically the same.

There is also a bass-relief from the ruins of Babylon, with a dog represented upon it, which is found by naturalists to be identical with a species of the dog existing in Asia at the present day.

Evidence of Fossil Remains

But we have still more conclusive evidence than this derived from ancient monuments of the very great permanence of the characteristics by which different species of plants and animals are distinguished from each other, in the fossil remains which exist in the strata of the earth. By means of these our observations upon the forms of vegetable and animal life which have existed upon our globe may be carried back to an immense antiquity, and extended over so vast a number and variety of species as to furnish us, as it has always been supposed, with all the means of information on this subject that can be desired. It has been thought to be fully proved by these observations that every species which exists upon the earth remains unchanged so long as it exists. When at length its period has expired, it disappears from the field, while new ones are continually arising to take the place of those that are gone. But no one passes, by gradations, into any other; and the lines of distinction by which each is separated from all the rest remain sharp and well-defined from the beginning to the end.

Opinions of Naturalists and Philosophers

At least, this has been hitherto the view which naturalists and philosophers have almost unanimously taken of this subject, though there have not been wanting writers who have maintained the contrary opinion. Notwithstanding the evidence furnished by the appearance of fossil remains, that the lines of demarcation separating the different species are absolutely and forever impassable, there have been some advocates of the theory that all the present races of animals may have been derived by insensible gradations from a few primordial types. This theory has very recently been brought forward anew in a form to attract general attention. Still, so unanimous and so decisive has been the testimony of geologists in respect to the evidence furnished by the fossil remains, and so inconsistent is it with the development theory, as it is called, that very great changes must take place in the opinion of naturalists in respect to the true import of the geological records before this opinion can be generally received.

But however the great question in respect to the absolute and perpetual permanence of the distinction of species may be ultimately decided, there is no doubt that all naturalists fully concur in the opinion that this permanence is, at all events, so great as entirely to preclude the possibility that the American species of plants and animals can have descended from the stocks of the old world within so short a period as six thousand years. Some other supposition must, therefore, be made than that the forms of life existing here could have been derived, within that period, by ordinary generation from those prevailing in other portions of the world. Some of the principal suppositions which have been made will be presently alluded to.

Examples of Diversity

Some of the American plants and animals attracted great attention in Europe when they were first made known there, being recognized as entirely new, and found to be quite peculiar in character. The potato was one; the turkey was another. No turkey was ever known to exist in Europe, Asia, or Africa before that time, and no fossil remains of such an animal have ever been discovered there. The tobacco plant was another species that was originally first found in America, though it has since become extensively diffused throughout the world. A more particular account of some of these plants and animals will be given in future chapter. They are only mentioned here as illustrations of the great truth, that when this country was first explored by European visitors an entirely new series of forms of vegetable and animal life was found to prevail here, and such as could not have resulted from any of the forms that prevail in the old world, within the period of six thousand years, through the operation of any laws that are known to us, in respect to the relation of parent and offspring.

The General Types the Same

And yet, though the plants and animals that are found in America are all different, and seem to be essentially different, so far as relates to derivation from the same parentage within any moderate period, from those of the old world, it is a very curious and a very significant fact, that there is a very close analogy between the two great stocks — an analogy so close as to furnish very strong reason to believe that they must have had a common origin, or at least have derived their existence from some common law. All, or nearly all, the great types of animal and vegetable life which are known in the old world, have their representatives in the new, and yet no particular species are so represented. While there is a generic similarity, there is also a specific difference. We scarcely knew which excites most our wonder and curiosity, the analogy in the great types, or the total, or almost total diversity in individual species. We say almost total, for, in addition to the exceptions already referred to, by the time that the fauna and flora of America came to be fully examined, great numbers of animals had been brought over, either by accident or design, from Europe, and mingled with the animals in America; and there are many plants which are now found growing wild in various parts of the country, and seem to be natives, but which are identical in species with those growing in Europe. It is inferred in such cases that the seeds were originally brought from the old world, though perhaps it cannot in all cases be positively proved that they were. It may however be said with certainty, that, as a general rule, of the hundreds and thousands of plants and animals, natives of America, that have been examined and described, all or nearly all are essentially different from those of corresponding type produced by the old world.

The accompanying engravings, which represent the gigantic vultures which inhabit the mountain summits respectively of the new world and the old, strikingly illustrated this principle. While they are generically similar, both in their structure and in their habits, still, in respect to what the naturalists call specific characters, they are entirely distinct.

The Mystery General

The mystery which attends the origin of these different and peculiar species of plants and animals inhabiting the new continent, has been found, since America was discovered, to be general, for it is now known that not merely America, but also every part of the globe, so far as the different zones and districts of the earth are separated from each other by seas, or mountains, or other great natural boundaries, has each its own fauna and flora different from those of every other region. These differences of species, too, exist not in space only, but in time. From the evidence that an examination of the strata of the earth affords, we find that every different period of the earth's history, going back to very remote ages, had its own system of plants and animals, so that thousands of species that existed once do not exist now, and those which exist now did not exist then. Thus it is established by evidence that seems to be conclusive, that just as in the history of any one species, there is a succession of individuals, each of which is born, grows, flourishes, declines, and dies, to be succeeded by others which rise into being, and come forward to maturity, while their predecessors decline; in the same manner, in the history of the world, there has been a succession of species. each of which has come into being in its own time, increased in numbers, become widely extended, and then has gradually diminished and finally. disappeared, to be succeeded by other species that arise in the same manner, and go through in the same manner the successive periods of youth, maturity, and decay. Thus it would appear that, of the vast congeries of animal and vegetable creations which the history of the globe presents to view, each separate period of its existence, and also every different district on its surface, has received its own peculiar and exclusive forms. There are several different opinions in regard to the proper explanation of this remarkable fact. Of these opinions only two are now seriously entertained by naturalists and philosophers, and the question between these two is, at the present time, a subject of earnest discussion throughout the whole scientific world.

The Two Principal Theories

The first opinion is, that each species is, in its essential nature, and has been throughout its whole history, entirely distinct from every other one, and that it was called into being in its own appointed time, either by a special act of creation exerted for this end, or else by the operation of some general laws to us wholly unknown, by which, when certain conditions are combined, a new species is derived in some mysterious way from one or more other species existing before it, just as individuals of any given species are known to proceed from other individuals of the same. This opinion has been hitherto a prevailing one among naturalists and philosophers, and a great desire has been felt to discover the general conditions and laws, if such there are within the reach of human observation, under which new species arise.

The second opinion is, that life, in all its manifestations, throughout the whole vegetable and animal world, is one, and that all organizations that now exist, or have ever existed, have been produced, by a succession of exceedingly gradual and long-continued changes, from one, or at most a very few, primordial forms.

These changes, it is supposed, result from a constitution of vegetable and animal life such that very slight modifications of structure occur in all cases in the descent from parent to offspring; that these modifications, which are insignificant, and sometimes scarcely perceptible in the first generation, become very great by being accumulated in a long series of years, and that changes thus resulting, branching off in different directions, as it were, according as the conditions and influences to which different races are exposed, vary, in different places and time, and acting through immensely long periods of time, have given rise to all the countless forms of animal and vegetable life with which the world now teems.

Inquiries Into This Subject Right and Proper

This is not the place to discuss, nor even to explain these opinions. They are only briefly alluded to here, on account of the bearing of this general question on the origin of life in America. Some persons feel a degree of hesitation in following the guidance of naturalists in their inquiries in respect to the laws of life, as if the object of those engages in these studies was to discover some way of accounting for the works of creation without acknowledging the hand of a creator. But this is not so. Scientific inquiries into the causes of what we see are not attempts to dispense with a divine agency in nature, but to discover the manner in which this agency is exercised, and the laws by which it regulates it action. When Franklin, and the other philosophers of his time, made known to the world that they had discovered the cause which produced thunder and lightning, many people thought it was impious for them to pretend to have done so. For the philosophers to attribute a phenomenon which had always been regarded as produced directly by the power of God to petty secondary causes, which they had themselves discovered, was, in the opinion of these persons, atheistical and profane.

But it is now universally admitted that such a discovery does not limit or control the power of God at all. It only enables us to see somewhat further into his ways. No one detracts from the honor due to an engineer for any grand result that he produces, by explaining the mystery of the secret mechanism that he has contrived by which to produce it.

It is so with all the works of nature. We may push our inquiries in every direction with the utmost diligence and vigor, and carry them to any extent, without the least fear of ever making any discoveries which will tend in the smallest degree to supersede the agency of a supreme and all-pervading power, either in the original constitution of nature, or in the constant control of all that takes place under the operation of its laws.

The Testimony of Scriptures

There is another source of apprehension, of a religious nature, by which the mind is sometimes restricted and hampered in studying the laws of nature and the past history of the globe, and that is the fear that something will be found which may conflict, or at least appear to conflict, with the testimony of Scripture, and thus shake the foundation of our Christian faith. But we must consider that the book of revelation is intended to instruct us solely in moral and spiritual truths, while the book of nature has been opened before us to teach us science and philosophy. They are both equally from God. In one as much as in the other, it is his voice that we hear, and his instructions that we receive; and we must not allow our ears to be closed, or our reason to be trammeled, in respect to what he teaches us directly in one, by too literal interpretations of what is said incidentally and indirectly in the other. Since the great mistake which was made in the time of Galileo, when it was attempted to shut out from mankind the evidences presented by mathematics and astronomy, in respect to the laws of the solar system, by inferences ignorantly drawn from incidental allusions in the Scriptures to the motions of the heavenly bodies, all wise and good men have come to the conclusion that we must look to the word of God for instruction in moral and religious truth alone, while for science and philosophy we must go to that other volume — the great system of creation and providence — which the same infallible teacher has spread open before us. Each comes from the same hand, and each in its own sphere it, in a certain sense, equally, for us, the word of God.

Means of Transportation for Animals and Plants

A great many very curious modes by which plants and animals may be transported from one country to another, even across wide and deep seas, have recently been brought to light, which very much diminish the difficulty of supposing that America might have been stocked from the old — provided always, we grant that plants and animals are subject to extensive modifications in the course of long periods of time, by which the species is finally changed, and new forms adapted to new situations and conditions are developed.

In the first place, the sea, instead of lying motionless, except so far as it is agitated by winds, as is often supposed, is subject to a great number and variety of currents, flowing in all directions, many of them at the rate of from twenty to sixty miles a day. These currents convey fields of ice, masses of drift wood, branches of trees with nuts, fruits, or other capsules containing seeds attached to them, and the bodies of dead birds, with seeds in their crops. There are many savage nations, living in countries that produce no trees, that depend on drift wood altogether for all the material of this sort that they use in making utensils and weapons, and even sometimes for building and for fuel. Now, the trunk of a single tree might contain the seeds and eggs of a hundred different species of minute plants and animals, and though great numbers would doubtless perish, many would probably be preserved.

Experiments have recently been made to ascertain how long seeds can remain submerged in sea water without losing their power of germination, and it was found that out of many hundreds subjected to the trial quite a large number grew after being in the water from twenty to ninety days. This would give them time to be conveyed a great distance by a current of the sea flowing at the rate even of twenty-five miles a day.

A certain philosopher wishing to ascertain how far aquatic birds might convey seeds from one lake or pond of fresh water to another, in the mud adhering to their feet, took out a portion of such mud, in order to ascertain how far it might be supplied with the germs of vegetable life. The quantity which he took was about a tea-cup full. This mud he placed in a situation to allow the seeds which it contained to germinate, and as fast as little plants appeared he pulled them out and counted them. He obtained from this single tea-cup full of soil more than two hundred living plants! Thus great numbers of transfers of plants from one region to another are doubtless made, merely by the feet of aquatic birds.

In a somewhat similar manner the young of many small animals are conveyed from lake to lake and from river to river, by attaching themselves to the feet and legs of birds, floating or wading in the water.

A great many other curious examples like these of the manner in which nature has provided for the wide dissemination of the minuter forms of animal and vegetable life might be given if time and space would allow.

Glacial Action

Whenever the temperature of a country, either from its great elevation or from its high latitude, is such that the summer cannot thaw the snow and ice which the winter produces, what are called glaciers are formed. These glaciers are beds of solid ice, of many hundred feet in thickness, which are formed in valleys or upon broad slopes of land, and which all the time slowly move down the descent upon which they lie, as if there were a certain slight and imperfect fluidity in the constitution of the ice. When such a glacier has it lower termination in a valley it sometimes ploughs up the ground before it, and deposits stones, which it has brought down upon its surface, in a particular way, and produces other curious effect, the results of the glacial action, by which the geologists feel confident that they can determine, upon a proper examination of any district or valley, whether or not a glacier has ever been at work there.

When these glaciers terminate upon the shore of the sea, the lower edge is forced out over the water by the pressure of a mass above and behind, until the projecting mass, sometimes many hundred feet in thickness, is broken off, falls over, and is borne away by the current or the wind, This is the way in which the immense icebergs that are seen floating about even in the middle of the ocean are formed.

The Glacial Period of North America

It is alleged by geologists that there are abundant evidences of former glacial action throughout all the northern and central parts of North America, and also of Europe and Asia, indicating that at some remote period the climate in all the northern latitudes was very much colder than it is now. Indeed, some astronomical arguments have recently been advanced showing that the earth, by the laws of its motion round the sun, which lead to a change in the position of its axis in relation to the sun, is subject to certain grand oscillations of temperature, in which the regions of the north and of the south poles are alternately made warmer and colder, and that at the present time the condition of the north pole is intermediate between the two extremes. However this may be, there are undoubted geological proofs that in former ages the northern countries, both of the old continent and the new, have been at one period much colder, and at another much warmer, than at present. When the climate was colder the reign of ice in all the northern regions, and the influence of it in connecting continents and transporting animals and men, would be of course greatly increased. If now we suppose that at such a time great numbers of the then existing species of animals were transported across the intervening seas, and then gradually spread themselves southward, undergoing slow modifications as they advance, to fit them for the new conditions to which the changes of the climate or their own changes of habitation exposed them, we should have very nearly the result which is now observed to exist.

These ideas, however, are, after all, at present only the speculations of naturalists and philosophers, ingenious and interesting as they are.

FACE OF THE COUNTRY

The Map

The map on the adjoining page represents the portion of the North American continent which is at the present time occupied by the people of the United States. It will assist very much in reading intelligently the history of the country if we first obtain a clear and comprehensive view of the great and leading features of its geography.

These features are very marked and striking — more so, perhaps, than those of any other country on the globe. This will clearly appear by an inspection of the map, and by filling out, in imagination, the outline which the map presents, with the details which will be given in this description.

As you look upon the map imagine that you are in the air, looking down upon it as from a balloon, and take notice of what you see. On the east and on the west are the shores of two oceans, That on the east is the Atlantic. The Pacific is on the west.

The Lake Country.

Toward the north is an immense tract of nearly level land, covered with forests, but containing a vast number of depressions in the surface of the land, all of which are filled with water and form lakes, some large and others small. This land, though level, is high, so that there is a very considerable though gradual descent from the lakes to the ocean. The lakes are kept constantly full by the rains and by the melting of the snows, and the surplus waters flow off in one vast channel, northward and eastward to the sea.

One of the large lakes, though still much higher than the sea, is marked as a low lake, for it is two or three hundred feet below the level of the others, and the water flowing from the upper lakes into it, in descending from one level to the other, passes over a high precipice, thus producing an immense fall, which is the celebrated Niagara.

The surplus waters of all the large lakes flow off finally in a northeasterly direction, almost exactly parallel to the coast until they reach the sea. The river thus formed is now known as the St. Lawrence. Observe, that between the river and the coast there is a long and somewhat narrow strip of land, which will be spoken of more particularly under another head.

All this region of the lakes is inhabited — during the summer season by immense numbers of beasts upon the land, of birds in the regions of the air, and of fishes in the water. In the winter it is buried deep in ice and snow. The birds at that season have all flown. The animals have retired to dens and holes, where some sleep, torpid, till the spring returns, and others burrowing beneath the frosty covering which clothes the ground, gain their livelihood there by digging for roots, or gnawing the bark of trees, or catching the fish that are still swimming in the imprisoned waters.

Fur-Bearing Animals

Almost all the land animals that inhabit these regions — being exposed for six months in the year to intense cold — are protected by a thick and warm coat of hair and fur. In the larger animals the hair is coarse, but thick and warm, though much less so than in the case of the smaller animals; for the smaller the body is that is exposed, the more perfect the protection that it requires, one large mass being more easily kept warm than a multitude of small ones.

The region of these lakes, and of the country north of it, which, for many hundreds of miles, maintains the same character, is one of the most extensive and most celebrated fur-bearing districts in the world. The shores of the lakes, and the banks of all the millions of little brooks and streams, are full of minks, otter, beavers, sables, and multitudes of other swimming and burrowing animals of that kind, whose fur is softer than silk and warmer than wool. When, therefore, you look upon the map and imagine that your eyes are surveying the real country, you must picture it to your mind as swarming with all this life, winter and summer.

In the summer these animals ramble about in the forests, or along the borders of the lakes and streams, amid a profusion of the most luxuriant and most beautiful flowers. Some climb the trees, and run along upon the branches in search of nuts for their winter stores. Some burrow in the ground, at the margin of the water, with the orifices of their dwelling convenient either for foraging upon the land, or for fishing and swimming in the ponds and streams.

The Indian Inhabitants

There is one thing more to be brought to mind in order to complete the picture, and that is, the presence of many wandering tribes of Indians roaming over the country. The smokes from their scattered wigwams rise among the trees both in summer and in winter.

They build their habitations of the bark of trees. They hunt and trap the land animals, and snare the fish. They eat the flesh for food, and clothe themselves with the skins and furs. Each tribe preserves in a measure its own range, and yet sometimes they become involved in dreadful quarrels, in which the ordinary repose of the silent and solitary forests is broken by the frightful yells of a troop of maddened savages breaking at midnight into the encampment of their foes, or by the piercing cries of women and children whom they massacre in their fury.

Influence of the Moral Instincts

These scenes of war and devastation are, however, only incidental and occasional interruptions to the ordinarily peaceful flow with which the current of life here, as in all other countries and climes, flows on. The Creator has implanted in the human mind a natural sense of justice, a love of what is right in the dealings between man and man, and a disapproval of what is wrong, the influence of which, in all human communities, is ordinarily sufficient to preserve peace, even in the most rude and savage states of society. Thus, in picturing to our imaginations the scenes that were presented in this lake country, while in its aboriginal condition, we must conceive of the inhabitants as ordinarily employed in their various industrial pursuits of hunting and fishing, of fabricating implements and clothing, of building wigwams and making encampments, and of rearing their children. The scenes of violence and war that occurred to disturb the usual quite of their lives, through very serious in their results, were exceptional, and comparatively rare. It is very doubtful, indeed, whether they were more frequent, or more destructive, in proportion to the numbers affected by them, than the similar quarrels which have occurred among Christian and civilized nations, as shown by the history of Europe during the last five hundred years.

The Great Central Valley

South of the lake country, and occupying a very large portion of the whole interior of the continent, is a broad though shallow valley, bounded both on the east and on the west by ranges of mountains. The extent of the valley is marked on the map, not only by the mountains which bound it on the east and on the west, but also by the ramifications of the great river which drains, it. These ramifications are seen spreading in every direction, like the branches of a mighty tree, and terminating in the south in one great trunk, through which the united volume of waters is poured out into the great gulf which is seen delineated there. This is the great river Mississippi, with its thousand tributaries. If is were the real scene, instead of a mere map that we were looking upon, we should see all the branches of this immense system glistening in the sun between banks loaded with luxuriant forests, and adorned with fruits and flowers of every conceivable character and form.

The Soil of the Great Valley

The soil of the whole valley, which, however, is so broad and so shallow that, seen as we have imagined from above, it would have more the appearance of an extended plain than of a valley, is extremely fertile. It is what is called an alluvial formation; that is, a very large portion of the territory has been covered with deposits from the rivers themselves, left after overflows and inundations. These deposits have accumulated, in the course of ages, to a great depth, and they form an exceedingly rich and fertile soil. The rivers twist and turn this way and that in meandering through these plains; and when swollen by rain or by the melting snows, they undermine the banks, and bring down great masses of earth, and great numbers of immense trees into the water. The earth thus washed in is carried down by the flood, and after being mingled with a great variety of animal and vegetable remains, is distributed over widely extended districts below, when the water has overflowed the banks, and thus adds, throughout all the country so covered, a new layer of fertility to the soil.

Formation of Islands in the River

The trees float on, too, upon the current. Some drag by the roots and get lodged along the banks or upon shoals, in the bed of the stream. In this latter case they intercept others coming down, and so create an obstruction, around which sand and sediment collect, until an island is formed. When this new formation becomes consolidated, it turns the current of the steam, and perhaps in the end is the means of deflecting the river into a new channel.

There is another way by which islands are formed. The river wearing continually upon its banks, and making immense convolutions in its course, sometimes cuts through a narrow neck, where previously it flowed around in a great circuit. A new channel is thus made for a part of the water, while the rest flows on round the circuit in the old course. By this means an island is formed, which may, perhaps, continue for centuries to divide the stream.

Swamps

At length, perhaps in the case of such an island, the old channel becomes choked up and closed at the opening, having previously become half filled with the floating trunks of trees, and all manner of brush and rubbish. Henceforward it remains a stagnant pool, a mile perhaps wide, and fifty miles long, filled with aquatic plants of every kind, and with decaying and half sunken trunks of trees, all covered and adorned, where they emerge into the atmosphere, with rich mosses, green and brown, and with graceful ferns, which hang drooping like tufts of feathers along the bands, or clinging, wherever they can get a foothold, to the trunks of the decaying trees.

The lagoons and morasses formed in this manner, in ancient times, became the peaceful and happy abode of vast numbers of animals adapted to such a habitation. Alligators, lizards, serpents, and reptiles of all kinds, crawled along the banks or slept in the sun upon the logs that line the shore; while long-legged birds waded in the water fishing for their food among the sedges, and flocks of ducks and other wild fowl, some of them resplendent in plumage, and adorned with the most gorgeous hues or orange, crimson, blue and gold, lay floating on the surface, or flew in flocks hither and thither through the air. The lagoons and morasses were inhabited by these animals in millions.

the Old Forsaken Channels

In other parts of this great valley swamps and morasses were formed in another way. The river, when it overflowed its banks, carried over with it, upon the land, immense quantities of sand, gravel, and driftwood, and other such substances, whether floating upon the water or suspended in it. These substances would, of course, be caught and retained, or, if heavier than the water, would subside in greater quantities near the bank than further inland; that is, the largest and heaviest would become lodged, while the water itself, carrying with it the finer sediment, would flow further into the interior. Thus the land would become built up, so to speak, faster near the river than further inland, and consequently would rise higher; and the water which was carried over into the plains beyond could not flow back into the river again. Instead of this, it would find its way into every low and sunken tract, which would, of course, in this way become half submerged, and long before the water could be evaporated by the sun a new supply would come in from another inundation.

The result is, that throughout the whole extent of the valley, especially in the southern and lower portions of it, great tracts of land have become half submerged, and continue permanently in that condition, and thus, though teeming with animal and vegetable life, are wholly unfit, in their present state, for the abode of man.

The Mouth of the Mississippi

The mouth of the river, as might be expected from the prevailing character which it bears throughout its course, presents a very extraordinary spectacle. The torrents that come down in the great floods bring with them vast numbers of trees and immense quantities of brush and drift wood, and also of sand and mud held in suspension by the water, all of which are swept out in every direction around the mouth of the river and deposited there. In this way, in process of time, a delta, or projection of the land has been formed, which is so large as to be plainly perceptible upon the map. This land rises scarcely above the level of the sea, and the water of the river makes its way through it in every direction, in many different and devious channels. The whole tract is, in fact, an entangled mass of trees and brushwood, matted together and gone to decay, and covered with mud and slime; and so unfit for the habitation of man that when, on the coming of the Europeans, a landing-place was required on the bank of the river; it was found necessary to ascend more than one hundred miles before a site suitable for a town could be found. And even at that spot the surface of the river is now often higher than the streets of the town which has been build there, and in digging a foot or two anywhere in the soil we come to the water.

The Prairies

In the northern part of this great fertile basin, watered by the Mississippi and its branches, there is a vast extent of country void of forests, or nearly void of them, there being no wood upon it except narrow belts of trees growing along the margins of the rivers. This country consists of boundless plains of grass land, called prairies. The soil is very fertile, and the grass grows high; and when from any small elevation the traveler takes a survey of the scene, looking out, as he may, to an unobstructed horizon on every side, and seeing the grass waving in the wind throughout the whole expanse around him, he might well imagine himself in the midst of an ocean — only that the billows that roll over it are green instead of blue. These plains, in aboriginal times, furnished food for buffaloes, elks, antelopes, and other animals that feed on herbage, the whole mass moving continually to and fro over the vast expanse as the season changed, or as the state of the pasturage invited them to new fields.

The Northern Atlantic Slope

The most important part of the whole territory represented on the map, in a historical point of view, is the Atlantic slope, as it is called — that is, the portion of the country between the mountains bordering the valley of the Mississippi, on the east, and the sea. You will see by the map that this is a long and narrow strip of land. It is divided naturally into two portions. The stormy cape which is seen projecting into the sea about midway of the coast marks this division. To the northward of this there is a tract of land lying between the sea on the one hand, and the river which carries off the surplus water of the great lakes on the other. This is the northern part of the Atlantic slope, and it was the scene of many of the most interesting events connected with the history of the country.

The country in this district is mountainous or hilly in every part. In former times it was covered with forests, except where the Indians had cleared small patches of ground, by burning down the trees, to make fields for the cultivation of maize. This tract of land was exactly adapted by nature for producing the grasses and other herbaceous plants, which form the food of the sheep, the horse, the ox, and other such grazing animals — the most useful of all to man. But no such animals were produced in this region. It would be impossible, indeed, that they should live here, in a state of nature, on account of the fact that, though in summer everything is favorable for the production of their food, in the winter, which season here lasts from four to six months in the year, the whole country is buried under the snow, and, of course, all such animals, if any there were, would perish.

Such animals are now, however, raised in great numbers in all this region. Indeed, they are the great staple of production. They feed themselves during the summer season from the grass that grows upon the hill-sides and upon the mountain slopes; while such as grows on the more smooth and level lands below is husbanded for them by the farmer, by being cut, and dried, and stored in barns, and so fed out to them under shelter during the winter season, when the fields and hill-sides are all alike buried under four or five feet under the snow.

Native Animals

Thus, in its native state, there were no animals in this region except such as could provide themselves with food, or live without it during the protracted winters. The moose, with his long legs to wade through the snow, and his long neck and head to reach up to the branches of the trees and under wood, could live by browsing upon the buds and the tender bark which grows upon them. The squirrels and other such smaller animals were endowed with instincts which led them to lay up food for the winter in hollow logs or holes in the ground. The bears went into a torpid sleep in which they remained insensible and without food for months at a time, and the minks and other burrowing creatures of that kind continued their operations under the ice and snow all winter long, feeding on roots or on fish; and whatever might be the severity of the cold above, finding it always warm and comfortable for them below.

Man

This northeastern region had its human inhabitants, too, notwithstanding the depth of the snow which covered it, and the intensity of the cold which prevailed during so large a part of the year. These inhabitants easily provided themselves with food during the summer season, partly by hunting and fishing, and partly by cultivating the ground in such spots as they had been able to clear of trees. They had a double resource in winter, too. In the first place there were the stores of provisions which, like the squirrels, they had laid up in the season of abundance, and then, even in the winter, the supplies which nature afforded them were not wholly cut off. For, although all above the surface of the earth, both of land and water, formed one lifeless and desolate expanse of frost and ice and snow, and was enveloped in an atmosphere so intensely cold that no active vegetable or animal life could endure exposure to it, still beneath this surface, both upon the land and upon the water, there was a protected stratum teeming with life in every form, and there were a thousand ways which their savage ingenuity devised of penetrating to this stratum, and drawing from it at least a portion of their needed supplies.

All this, however, will be more fully explained in a subsequent chapter.

The Southern Atlantic Slope

To the south of the stormy cape represented on the amp, and between the mountains and the sea, is the southern Atlantic slope, of nearly the same size and form as its northern counterpart, but extremely dissimilar in character. It consists mainly of level plains, covered, in a great measure, with forests of pine; and across these plains innumerable rivers flow from the mountains to the sea, through valleys of the most extraordinary richness and beauty. In this country the grasses do not grow,, but their place is filled by tropical plants. The two chief plants that have been cultivated here are rice and cotton.

Character of the Coast

One very curious and extremely important result of the difference of the conformation of the land in the northern and southern portion of the Atlantic slope, is a great difference in the accessibility of the coast in the two sections. Where a district of country is mountainous and rocky, the shores are usually bold, and the indentations in the land are filled with deep water. The rivers, too, in flowing through such a country, are bounded generally by steep and permanent banks, which yield but little sand or soil, to be borne away by the current of the stream. The rivers are consequently more likely to be deep, and their mouths to be comparatively unobstructed.

On the contrary, where a coast is low and sandy, it is undermined and washed away by the waves, and shoals and sandbars and low islands are formed all along the line of it. The rivers, too, in flowing through such a country, undermine and wear away the banks, and bring down great quantities of sand and gravel to fill the beds of the rivers, and choke up the entrances at their mouths.

These causes operate powerfully in the two portions of the eastern coast of this country. The shores in the northern portion are bold and permanent, and almost every considerable indentation in them forms a deep and safe harbor for shipping. In the southern portion, on the other hand, the coast is lined with shoals and sandy islands; and although there are numerous inlets and bays between and among them, they are almost all shallow, and the approaches to them are choked up with continually shifting sands.

It is so with the rivers. The Hudson river has one-third greater depth of water at its mouth than the Mississippi, although the Mississippi reckons twice as many thousands of miles as the Hudson hundreds, in its length, and discharges, doubtless, into the sea, judging from the area which it drains — more than a hundred times the quantity of water.

From these causes the northern coast is much more accessible to ships coming from sea than the southern, and to this advantage, doubtless, and to the facilities for commerce resulting from it, it is owing, in some considerable degree, that so many early settlements were made on the shores of the northeastern slope, and that the section of country lying contiguous to them has made such rapid advances in wealth and population.

The Western Slope

If we pass now across the country to the western slope, we see a range of mountains running parallel with the coast at a comparatively short distance from the sea. This chain of mountains was named by the Spaniards who first explored the country the Sierra Nevada, which means snowy chain. The strip of land which lies between these mountains and the sea is too narrow to produce any considerable rivers. One, however, is seen crossing the chain of mountains, flowing through a gap or gorge, left, it would almost seem, on purpose to allow a passage. The mouth of this river forms a deep and spacious harbor, the only one of importance upon the coast. It is this harbor that has given rise to the city of San Francisco.

The Great Salt Desert

There remains one more district, and that a most remarkable one, to be described. It is the great desert which lies between the Snowy Chain and the range of mountains which bounds the Mississippi on the west. The desert character of this tract arises, it would seem, from the scarcity of rain, and from the sandy and porous character of the soil, which causes all the water that falls upon it to be absorbed so suddenly that it cannot serve the purposes of vegetation. Streams rise in the mountains around it, and some of them, by the confluence of tributaries, become quite large rivers in going down into the valley. But in flowing over the great sandy waste which here receives them, the water is rapidly absorbed. The streams grow smaller and smaller as they go on, and finally disappear. In the spring of the year, when the snows melt, or in times of great rains, these rivers are swollen so as to extend in length a hundred miles or more, but even at such times they finally dwindle away and disappear.

Some of the rivers, however, before they disappear, reach great hollows or depressions in the land, which depressions, of course, they fill, and thus are formed lakes. The smaller of these lakes, in summer, dry up and disappear, leaving only salt incrustations upon the ground; others being larger, are permanent. There is one, the Great Salt lake, which is some hundreds of miles in extent. The water from these permanent lakes is, of course, all the time infiltrating into the sand below, and evaporating into the air above, but before the whole quantity is exhausted, the rains upon the mountains send down a fresh supply, and thus the vast reservoir is never wholly emptied.

The Deposits of Salt

There is one very curious phenomenon which occurs throughout this region, and that is the tendency to deposit salt, which the waters indicate. The great lake, as its name denotes, is salt, and saline incrustations are found upon the ground in various places where lakes and pools have dried away. It is found to be a general law, though perhaps not universal, that wherever lakes exist that are fed by rivers or other streams flowing over the surface of the ground — and not by springs — and which have no outlet to the sea, they are salt. There may be exceptions, but this is the general law.

For a long time the cause of this phenomenon was enveloped in great mystery, but this mystery has at length been solved. It is found that the earth contains, and continually produces saline substances in the soil. The rain falling upon a district of country dissolves a portion of these substances, and they are borne away by the water into brooks and streams. The quantity is too small to affect the taste of the water while it is in this condition, and so we call the water fresh, and it continues fresh until it reaches the sea.

If, however, it never reaches the sea, but like the water that comes down from the mountain sides into the great American desert it spreads itself out into lakes and pools, and there evaporates, the salt then becomes concentrated so as to manifest itself very decidedly to the taste, and to the other senses. For in the process of evaporation it is the water only that is taken up into the air. The saline particles which it contained are all left behind. Thus the saline element accumulates. Every fresh rain brings down an exceedingly small, it is true, but still an additional supply; and as nothing is taken away, the quantity, after the lapse of ages, becomes very great. The Dead Sea, which is isolated in this manner, and has been for thousands of years receiving a small continual supply from the saline substances which the Jordan and its branches have washed from the soil, has become more salt than the ocean.

The Diggers

The great desert valley which lies thus between the Rocky Mountains and the Snowy Chain of the Pacific, is not wholly desert and uninhabited. There are regions on the mountain sides and in the valleys in which a scanty vegetation thrives, and where reptiles and other animals of a humble order are produced. There are even tribes of Indians low and degraded enough to be fitted to these gloomy and desolate abodes. They are called Diggers, from the fact that they obtain their subsistence by digging into the ground for roots and for snails and reptiles of every kind.

Climate of the Country

For nearly six months of the year, throughout the whole breadth of the continent from east to west, the polar cold, following the sun as he withdraws during that season of the year beyond the equator to the south, comes down from the Arctic regions, and envelopes all the northern half of the country in ice and snow, and then, during the remaining six months, the returning sun brings back warmth, and with it spreads verdure and beauty again over the whole.

During the winter season, all along the northern frontier, the snow in the forests lies often for months at a time four and five feet deep, while the ice is at least half that thickness upon the rivers and ponds. The intensity of the cold of course rapidly diminishes in advancing to the southward, and along the southern frontier it is very seldom that either snow or ice is seen.

It is a singular circumstance that the difference of the temperature at the different seasons of the year is very much greater on this continent than on the other. There is about twice as great a difference between the average heat of summer and winter in Quebec as at Paris, it being here much warmer in the one season and much colder in the other. In Scotland the summers are not warm enough to ripen grapes or Indian corn, and yet in the winters the sheep can feed in their pastures almost without interruption during the whole year. In the corresponding region on this side of the Atlantic, while the rays of the summer sun are sufficiently concentrated and continuous to ripen the grapes and the corn, the winter's cold is so intense that, for six long months, the sheep and cattle have no access to the pasturage at all, the whole surface of the ground having become solid as a rock, and being also buried many feet under the snow.

Recapitulation

Look now once more upon the map and take a general survey of the country which it represents, by way of fixing the great leading features of it upon your mind. There is the lake country at the north, covered with forests, and the summit level occupied by four great inland seas, which pour their waters down over the precipice of Niagara into the lowermost lake, and thence flow off in a northeasterly direction into the ocean. South of this is the great Mississippi Valley, occupying almost the whole interior of the country, and displaying a vast net-work of rivers which, collecting the waters of the whole region, brings them all together into the center of the valley and carries them through one immense channel southward into the sea. By the side of this valley to the westward is a great dry and barren basin, bordered by mountains on every side, and with no rivers except such as are formed by streams coming down from the mountains after rains, or from the melting of the snows, and are soon absorbed by the thirsty sands. These two great basins occupy the center of the continent.

To the westward of them is the narrow strip which forms the Pacific slope, between the mountains and the sea, and to the eastward of them is the Atlantic slope, level and plain in the southern part, but mountainous and rugged toward the north.

These are the great leading features of the country, which it is necessary to keep distinctly in mind in studying its history.

REMARKABLE PLANTS

Distinction of Indigenous and Exotic

A plant that grows originally in any locality as a native of it is said to be indigenous to that locality. Those which have been brought to it by man, either by accident or design, are exotic. Thus the orange tree that grows in a pot or a tub in a lady's parlor in any northern part of America is an exotic; so is the wheat that grows in the farmer's fields — both plants having been brought to that locality by man. But the Indian corn, or maize, as it is more properly called is indigenous, that plant being, so far as is known, a native of the country.

Of the numerous plants found growing in America at the time it was discovered by Europeans, some very strongly resembled plants of the same class growing in the old world, though different in species from them. There were others, however, that possessed characteristics almost wholly new, and some of them soon began to attract great attention. Among these may be named the cotton plant, rice, the tobacco plant, the potato, and maize.

The Cotton Plant

Man is the only animal needing clothing that is not furnished with it by nature, but he is provided instead with the faculty of clothing himself, and one of the most striking of the marks of design, and of the adaptation of a want to a supply, which we find everywhere around us, consists in the provision which is made for furnishing him with materials for this work.

In all the cold regions of the earth there are the skins of beasts at hand in great abundance, covered with warm wool and fur, ready for his use. In all the warm regions are the cotton plants.

Many Species

There are a great many different species of cotton plants in the world, each great tropical district producing its own kind. These different species are very unlike in many respects, and cannot be changed into one another by the influence of climate or soil, or by different modes of cultivation. They all agree, however, in this, that when the seed is ripe the capsule bursts open, and presents a white fleecy tuft to view, inviting the naked savage, as it were, to come and spin and weave himself a garment with it.

Savages have in all ages and in every clime shown themselves ready to accept the invitation, and in Egypt and India, and in many tropical islands of the sea, cotton has been spun and woven from periods long antecedent to any records of history.

America, too, it was found, very soon after it was discovered, had its cotton plants, and cloth made from the little fleeces which they bore was worn by the natives in all the tropical regions. Specimens of the cloth have been found in some ancient tombs in South America, showing that it has been in use here from a very ancient period. In the colder regions the plant did not grow. Here the natives were compelled to content themselves with the skins of beasts, and with such fabrics as they could make from the fibrous bark of trees.

The name of the genus that comprises all the species of cotton plants is gossypium. Some of the species which were found in America proved to be superior to any others previously known. There is one species, in particular, which was found in some of the West India Islands, and was brought to the United States in 1786, and is now cultivated on the low and level islands lying along the southern coast, that we described in the last chapter, and which is far more valuable than any other found upon the globe. Its superiority consists in the fineness and softness and length of the fibre. It will not grow anywhere and retain its qualities except on, low rich land along the sea shore, and it thrives best upon the islands above referred to. It is called on that account sea island cotton.

The fibres of cotton, seen under a powerful microscope, appear like long ribbons, perfectly smooth and continuous from beginning to end. They are transparent, too, though the reflection of the light from so many countless millions of them when they lie together gives the whole mass a white appearance, just as a mist or fog appears white while the sun shines upon it, although it consists of millions of drops of perfectly pellucid water.

Cotton Intended for the Clothing of Men

It is not known that the tuft of cotton is of any advantage to the seed which it envelopes, or that it fulfills any other useful purpose in the economy of the plant. It would seem that it was expressly intended for the clothing of man, just at the fruits and the grains which other plants produce were intended for his food. There is this difference in the two cases, however, namely, that while the fruits and grains have a useful purpose to accomplish in respect to the plants which produce them, as well as being available for the purposes of man, the little fleece which envelopes the seed of the cotton plant seems, so far as we know, not be necessary to the plant at all, thus leaving us to infer that nature produces it with very special, if not exclusive, reference to the wants of man.

The birds in the countries where it grows make great use of it too to give a soft and downy lining to their nests.

Rice,

Several species of rice were found indigenous to America. Rice is the most productive food-bearing plant, for the use both of men and animals, that is known. It grows wild in the water in low and swampy lands along the borders of the rivers in tropical countries. Countless millions of birds gather over all the region where it grows in the season of its ripening, and multitudes of other animals, such as gain access to the ground when the water subsides, live upon it.

The Indians used to gather it by sailing in through the midst of it in their canoes, where bending down the heads of the rice, they would beat off the grains into the boat by means of a sort of threshing stick made for the purpose.

Maize

The most important and valuable plant, however, for the American Indians, especially for those who lived beyond the limits of the rice country, was the maize, or Indian corn. A great many of the tribes cultivated this plant in fields which they cleared for this purpose, by digging around the roots of trees and burning them off. Such fields were very numerous in the northern parts of the country when it was first discovered by white men., Indeed, this plant seems to have been their chief reliance for vegetable food. they considered it as the special gift of the great Spirit, and it figures very conspicuously in all their traditionary legends in respect to the creation of the world, and the early history of the human race.

An Indian Tradition

One of these legends is as follows: —
The first men who were created, says the tradition, proved to be bad men, and the great Spirit, finding them to be incorrigible, destroyed them all by drowning them in a great lake.

This story of the destruction of the first race of men by water is supposed to by some to have originated in a tradition of the general deluge described in the Sacred Scriptures.

After having thus destroyed one generation, the Great Spirit created another man, and finding, after he had lived alone for some time, that his condition was too solitary, he made him a sister. The brother and sister lived together quite happily for a while, when at last one morning the brother said that he had had a dream.

Five young men he saw in his dream, he said, coming one after another to see his sister, desiring her in marriage. She rejected the first four and accepted the fifth. This was a token, he thought, that if such young men should come she was to refuse the four first and accept the last. His sister said that she would do so.

In a short time the young men began to come. The first was named Tobacco. This was, however, before any such plant as tobacco was known. The young lady refused his suit, and he immediately fell backward and died. We use here the English names of the plants referred to. Of course in the original legend the Indian names are given.

Next came a young man named Bean. He, too, was refused, and fell back and died like the other.

The next one was named Pumpkin, and the next Melon. Thy both met with the same fate as their predecessors. All fell backward when they found themselves rejected, and died.

Finally the fifth young man came. His name was Maize. The girl smiled upon him, and gave him her hand. They were married, and from them proceeded all the subsequent generations of the human family.

From the ground where the bodies of the others lay buried there sprang up the several plants bearing these persons' names, the tobacco, the pumpkin, the melon, and the bean.

The narration of this legend here answers the double purpose of showing how important a place in the estimation of the Indians the maize plant occupied as an article of food for them, and also of giving an example of the traditionary tales which have come down from former generations in respect to the origin of the human family.

The Distinction of Exogenous and Endogenous

The maize plant brings to our view one of the greatest and most important distinctions that appear in the vegetable world, that of exogenous and endogenous plants, or, as they are sometimes termed, EXOGENS and ENDOGENS.

The word exogenous means outgrowing. An exogenous plant is one that grows by successive layers deposited at intervals beneath the bark upon the outside of the stem, as is the case with early all trees and shrubs that grow in cold or temperate climates. They all have a pith in the center and a bark upon the outside, and the wood of the stem between is formed by layers deposited in succession immediately beneath the bark.

An endogenous plant, on the other hand, grows by a uniform expansion of the whole substance of the stem within. It has no pith and no bark. The external surface is hard, however, and smooth. It is sometimes even glossy. The maize is perhaps the largest specimen of an endogenous plant which grows in northern latitudes. Very large specimens grow in tropical regions. The date, the bamboo, the rattan, the sugar cane, and various other canes, such as those used for fishing poles, are all endogenous. Indeed, this is the prevailing type of tropical vegetation, and the fact that maize is of this character seems to indicate that it is of tropical origin.

It is a very curious circumstance that the seeds of all exogenous plants have two lobes, while those of endogenous plants have only one. The lobes of a seed are by the botanists called cotyledons. Hence the class of endogens are sometimes called monocotyledonous plants, while that of exogens are called dicotyledonous. What connection there should be between the single cotyledon of the seed and the peculiar character and growth of the endogenous plant, its hard and shining outside surface, with no bark and no successive layers of wood, and on the other hand between a two-lobed constitution of the seed, and a bark, a pith, and a growth by successive outside layers, is a profound mystery. That there is some latent connection, however, is sure, for the two distinctions correspond with each other throughout the whole domain of the vegetable world.

In some plants, as in the bean, for example, the two cotyledons of the seed come out of the ground when the seed germinates, and appear above the surface in the form of two thick oval leaves. The division exists, though it is not so apparent in the seeds of all bark bearing trees, shrubs, and herbs of every kind.

The Tobacco Plant

Perhaps the most extraordinary of all the native American plants, considered in respect to the influence which it has exerted, and the effects which it has produced in the world since the discovery of America, is the tobacco plant. The attention of the Europeans was called to it almost from the outset. Columbus, when he first landed, sent some messengers into the interior on an exploring tour, and on their return, among other things that they reported, they said they found the natives smoking little rolls formed of the leaf of some sort of plant. One end of these rolls, they said, the people put into their mouths, and thus drew the smoke in from the other end which was lighted.

The plant was afterward found to be a narcotic, that is, to have the power of producing a sleepy and dreamy sensation when taken into the system. There are a great many plants produced in other parts of the world, the effects of which upon the system are narcotic, but those of the tobacco plant are peculiar. They are far more agreeable, and perhaps less injurious — so they say at least that use it — than those of any other narcotic plant.

It was, however, sixty or seventy years after the time that the attention of Columbus was first called to the plant before it was known in Europe. During all this time, though its existence and its effects were known to travelers visiting America, the use of it was regarded as a repulsive habit of savages, not to be imitated by civilized men. At length, in the year 1560, a small quantity of it was sent across the Atlantic to a certain Flemish merchant, and he sent a portion as a curiosity to the French minister at the court of Portugal, at Lisbon. The name of this minister was Nicot.

Nicot presented some specimens of the tobacco to the king of Portugal and to other distinguished personages, and they made trial of its effects. They were all so much pleased with the dreamy exhilaration which it produced upon them that they sent for more, and in this way it was soon introduced into Europe, where its fame spread with great rapidity. A very strenuous opposition arose to the use of it at the same time, and kings and governments, both civil and ecclesiastical, made earnest efforts to suppress it, but all in vain; and it has since, as is well known, become one of the most widely extended articles of consumption, and the most important in its effects, either for good or for evil, that the vegetable kingdom produces for man.

The Habit of Using Tobacco

This is not the place to discuss the character of these effects. All that I shall say is, that those who escape forming the habit of using tobacco in their youth, always, I believe, rejoice, through all the subsequent years of their lives, in their exemption from what is at best an inconvenience and a peril; while those who form the habit often spend their lives in fruitless and vexatious efforts to escape from the thralldom of it, and seldom or never recommend to others to follow their example in acquiring it.

Botanical Name

The botanists, when they came to procure specimens of the different species of the plant, and to add it to their catalogues, gave to the genus the name Nicotiana, from the name of the French minister, who was the first to bring it into notice in Europe. There is a substance, too, which is extracted from the plant, which has a name of the same derivation, Nicotine. Nicotine is very abundant in the leaves of the plant, and is one of the most virulent poisons known.

The potato

The potato is another very remarkable plant which was introduced into Europe from America, and which has exerted a vast influence — though in this case the influence is a wholly salutary one — upon the condition of mankind. It is supposed that by providing a cheap and abundant sustenance for the lower classes of people, it has actually added many millions to the population of Europe.

It came in the first instance from South America, and it is said that originally the tubers of the plant were very small, and far less nutritious than they are now. The change has been produced by cultivation. It is always found that when man selects any plant growing in a state of nature, and takes it under his care, with a view of using it for food, nature comes forward to meet him, as it were, and aid him in his effort, by giving the plant so chosen a new and fuller development in respect to the qualities which fit it for his purposes. Thus the apple, which was small, hard, and sour in its native woods, becomes large, tender, sweet and juicy when man chooses it for his food, and transfers it to his gardens. Similar changes take place in the grape, the peach, the pear, the potato, and in almost all other plants that produce food for man.

When, therefore, a new plant is discovered in some remote and partially explored country, it is not always easy at first to decide upon its value, for it is not known what effect cultivation will have upon it. There is a very important society in France, called the Society of Acclamation, the object of which is to bring new plants and animals from remote regions of the earth to Paris, with the view of ascertaining by experiment what the effect of a new climate and artificial culture will have upon them. Several important discoveries have already been made by this society, and it is prosecuting its researches with increased vigor, and on a more and more extended scale every year.

The potato met with almost as much opposition at its first introduction into Europe as tobacco. The opposition in this case, however, was found to be a prejudice, arising simply from the fact that the plant itself and the use of it for food were something new. The poor people especially would have nothing to do with it. It was a food fit only for beasts, they said, and they were determined that it should not be forced upon them. These prejudices have long since disappeared, and the once despised tuber is now a universal favorite all over the civilized world.

The Magnolia

When the European discoverers first landed upon the American shores, the grandeur and beauty of the native forests seem to have impressed them more than anything else that they beheld. Among the trees which chiefly contributed to this magnificence was the magnolia, which was found growing very profusely in all the southern regions of what now form the United States. Some species of this splendid class of plants grow in the Middle and even in the Northern States, but in this latter locality they are rare.

The magnolia grandiflora, so called, when in perfection, is one of the most magnificent trees in the world. It grows, it is said, sometimes to the height of seventy feet. It leaves are evergreen, and are polished on the surface, and at the proper season of the year the whole tree is covered with a profusion of immense white flowers, which bloom so conspicuously in the midst of the masses of verdure which surround them as to strike the eye of the stranger with wonder and delight.

There are a great many different species of the magnolia in America, which vary much in minor particulars, such as in the size of the plant itself and in the magnitude and fragrance of the flowers. There is one species which bears leaves two or three feet long, with flowers the cups of which are sometimes nearly a foot in diameter. The flowers of most of he species are very fragrant, some of them so much so that a tree, it is said, will scent the air for a distance of three miles. In some of the species the plants are small and shrub-like in form, but still producing flowers of extreme fragrance and beauty. There is one which is called the weaver laurel, which bears leaves and flowers of extreme elegance, and diffuses a fragrance so strong that it perfumes the atmosphere for a great distance around.

Since the discovery of America various species of the magnolia have been transplanted to Europe, and cultivated there in botanical gardens and in private pleasure grounds, where they are regarded as great curiosities. None of them were known in Europe until they were carried thither from America, but since that time it has been found that some species of the plant occur in China and Japan, though they are not identical with any of those found in the new world.

The Mahogany Tree

Next to the potato, which has so largely increased the means of sustenance for the masses of the population in Europe, and the cotton plant, which supplies so many millions with clothing, perhaps the most useful of the native productions of the American soil, in respect to the welfare and enjoyment of mankind at large, is the mahogany tree. This is a very large forest tree, which grows in vast numbers in the West India Islands and in certain parts of Central America. It is characterized by a certain combination of qualities which render it superior as a material for making furniture, and for cabinet work in general, to any other wood in the world. These qualities are its beautiful color, its hardness, making it susceptible of a fine polish, and the stability of its fibers, that is, its freedom from all tendency to warp, shrink, or split. It grows moreover in very massive trees, from which planks of almost any size may be sawed, and logs of it, containing vast quantities of the wood, can be cut and transported with great facility. Wood has thus sometimes been procured from a single tree to the value of four or five thousand dollars.

It was more than two hundred years after America was discovered before mahogany began to be introduced into Europe as an article of consumption, but now it is universally employed there, and the demand for it is so large that the British maintain extensive settlements in Honduras, solely for the purpose of cutting and shipping it.

The work of cutting the trees and floating them down the rivers to the sea is performed by the natives of the country, acting under the superintendence of Europeans. These natives work in gangs of thirty or forty together. When a tree has been selected to be felled, they build a staging against the side of it, ten or twelve feet from the ground — the part of the stem below that point not being valuable.

The tree is then cut through just above the staging, and when it has fallen the branches are lopped off, and the stem is divided into suitable lengths for convenient transportation. The logs are floated down the little streams on the banks of which they grew to the larger rivers, and are there made up into rafts, which, guided by skilled raftsmen, are carried down by the currents to the ports whence they are to be shipped to foreign countries. Some of the logs thus transported are of immense size and of great value.

Such are a few of the most characteristic and celebrated American plants that were brought to the notice of mankind after this continent was discovered. In the next chapter we shall consider some of the most remarkable animals.

REMARKABLE ANIMALS

The Beaver

One of the most remarkable of the animals found in America is the beaver. Species nearly resembling the American beaver formerly existed in the old world, but they have long been nearly or quite extinct. The class of animals to which the beaver belongs is common all over the world, namely, the class of Rodentia, which means gnawing animals. The beaver is the greatest gnawer of them all.

The Beaver's Teeth

His cutting teeth are broad and flat, and are brought to so sharp and hard an edge that the Indians were accustomed to set them in handles and use them for cutting instruments before they obtained iron and steel from the Europeans. It is said that by means of these teeth the beavers can cut off a stem in the woods as big as a walking stick at a single bite. By more continued efforts they can fell trees of very considerable size, not greater, however, than eight or ten inches in diameter, though one trapper in the service of a fur company says he has seen trunks eighteen inches in diameter cut through by them.

Fame of the Beaver

The beaver has acquired a very extensive fame among mankind, the foundation of which is two-fold. First, the exceeding softness and richness of his fur, which made his skin very valuable as clothing to the native tribes before Europeans came to the country, and which have since caused it to be still more highly valued by civilized nations all over the world; and secondly, his distinguished reputation as a builder. Both these characters of the animal result from the same cause, namely this, that he is intended to live in a very cold climate, that is, a climate which is very cold for half the year, and to get his living from the roots of plants growing under water, which, during the cold season, is covered with ice from one to three feet thick. To meet these exigencies he is provided with an extremely thick and soft fur to protect him in his winter excursions upon the land, and with certain very remarkable building instincts, by which he is enabled at all times, however cold the weather and however thick the ice, to procure access to the water.

His System of Building

The first object of the beaver in his engineering operations, is to keep the water deep in the stream that he inhabits, in order to prevent its freezing to the bottom. To effect this he forms a company, and the whole band proceed to build a dam. They gnaw down trees and bushes and drag them into the stream at the place which they have chosen for the dam, and pack them together in a close and impenetrable mass ten or twelve feet wide at the bottom, and diminishing gradually to the top. As they proceed they fill up all the interstices of the work with stones, gravel, mud, turf, roots, and everything else that they can bring. Of course a great deal of their work is washed away by the current while they are building, but by means of their indomitable perseverance, they finally succeed, and a massive and permanent obstruction to the stream is created. In process of time the trunks and stems of trees which they have introduced into their work decay, and the whole settles and consolidates into a permanent bank, which endures sometimes for centuries. Of course, so long as the pond is occupied the dam needs constant watching and frequent repairs, but this work the company always attend to in the most prompt and systematic manner.

In laying the materials of which the dam is composed the beavers go continually to and fro over the work, trampling down the soft substances with their paws, and patting them with their broad flat tails. This patting motion of their tails, which they make instinctively when they walk about upon the ground, gave rise to the story that the beaver uses his tail as a trowel. This, though it is not literally and exactly true, is, after all, not far from the truth, for the effect of the patting is analogous to that produced by the trowel of the mason in laying stones in mortar.

The House

Besides the dam, the beaver builds what may be called houses on the bank, where he can live during the winter sheltered from the cold, and protected from the wolves and similar wild animals that would otherwise prey upon him. These houses are built of logs of wood formed from the trunks of trees, which the beavers gnaw down in the adjoining forests, and then cut to proper lengths for their purpose. They dig in the ground to get good foundations, and then build up walls four or five feet high, much in the same way as they construct the dams. They then lay other trunks of trees across from one wall to the other, and cover the roof thus formed with stones, bushes, moss, mud, and other similar materials, and smooth the whole over at last with their paws and their tail, so as to make a sort of mound of their work, with a hollow in the center. The whole structure is so solid, and all its parts so closely compacted together, that the wolverines and wild cats cannot get in. It is very difficult even for men to break through such a sold mass.

From these habitations subterranean passages run in various directions — some opening into the pond under the ice, so as to afford the inhabitants free access and egress to the water at all times, and others lead to holes and caverns which the animals make as places of retreat from their enemies when they are alarmed, and perhaps for warmth in times of extreme cold.

Working Hours

It is a very curious circumstance that the beavers do all their work in the night, and thus no person can watch them at their operations except at a great disadvantage. In the day time they keep very quiet. Their motive, probably, in thus arranging their time, as far as action prompted by such animal instincts may be said to have a motive, is doubtless to avoid attracting the attention of their enemies.

The beavers were once very numerous throughout the whole northern portion of the territory now occupied by the United States. In all the settled parts of the country, however, they have nearly or entirely disappeared; and so valuable are their skins, and so closely do the hunters and trappers follow up the work of taking them, that it will not be many years, if the present state of things continues, before the whole race will be completely exterminated.

Other Fur-Bearing Animals

Besides the beaver, there are a great many other fur-bearing animals, such as the mink, the otter, the sable, and others that live on the banks of ponds and streams in America, and, like the beaver, seek their principal food in the water. There are none of them, however, that build either dams or habitations. Perhaps this is because they are smaller, and can more easily find space enough under the ice for their fishing and foraging excursions, without resorting to artificial means to keep up the water, and can also more easily find or make holes in the ground sufficient to furnish them a safe retreat from the cold, and a refuge from the hostility of their enemies.

These animals all produce fine and valuable furs, and are caught every winter by the trappers and hunters in great numbers, especially in that wide region of cold and desolate country which extends northward from the American frontier toward the pole, and which would be almost valueless to men, except for these productions.

Curious Phenomenon

There is one thing very curious about this class of animals that get their living in a great measure under water, and are consequently obliged to be often submerged, even in the coldest winter weather, and that is, that their fur becomes very little wet by such immersion. A dog, after plunging into a river, comes out wet to the skin, but the fur of a beaver or a mink, on account probably of some oleaginous substance with which it is dressed, does not allow the water to penetrate, so that, after swimming across a stream, or burrowing among roots at the bottom of a pond, the animal seeks the bank again, and comes out with only the outer surface wet, the skin beneath being as dry as when he went in. Thus, when swimming in the coldest water he is never cold.

The Buffalo

The buffalo, or bison, is a sort of wild bull, with a monstrous shaggy head and ferocious aspect. They are gregarious animals, that is, they live and feed together in immense herds. Almost all animals that feed on grass and herbage are gregarious, while beasts of prey are generally solitary in their habits. It is necessary for them to be so, for in order to succeed in their hunting, they must prowl about alone, or watch in ambush, patiently and in silence, for their prey. There are some exceptions, as in the case of wolves, for example, which usually hunt together in packs. There is a reason for this exception, too, for the wolves live generally by killing and devouring animals larger than themselves. and so are obliged to combine their strength in order to overpower their prey.

The buffalos are gregarious by habit in order that they may the better defend themselves from their enemies; and so abundant is the food furnished for them by the luxuriant grass of the prairies, and so boundless is the extent of the plains over which they roam, that the herds increase to an almost incredible extent. Travelers sometimes find the whole region black with them in every direction as far as they can see. In one case that is described, the country was covered with a herd, or an aggregation of herds, so vast that the party journeying were six days in passing through them. The aspect which they presented with five, ten, and sometimes twenty thousand in sight at a time, spreading in every direction over the plains, some bellowing, some fighting, others advancing defiantly toward their supposed foes, and tearing up the soil with their hoofs and horns — the earth trembling under their tramp, and the air filled with a prolonged and portentous murmur, presented to the view of the traveler a really appalling spectacle. the bellowing of a large herd is sometimes heard at a distance of two miles!

Annual Migration

Of course the frosts and snows coming down from the Arctic regions in winter bind up and cover large tracts of land which in summer are clothed with luxuriant herbage. The grazing animals, accordingly, move southward to great distances as the season changes. These migrations, in respect to the numbers and the sold mass of the moving columns, surpass in grandeur all other spectacles that the animal kingdom affords.

Swimming the Streams

The country being intersected by rivers and streams in every part, as shown by the map, would seem to interpose great difficulties in the way of the passage of the animals to and fro. The difficulties are great, but they are not insurmountable. The herd, on approaching a river, if it is fordable, descend the bank in a massive column, and wade or swim across. If the descent of the bank is not already gradual, it soon becomes so by the trampling of so many heavy hoofs, the most daring, of course, impelled partly by their courage and partly by the pressure from behind, going down first and breaking the way.

If there are calves in the herd, and the bank remains so steep that they dare not go down, their mothers always wait with them upon the margin, in great apparent distress, and make every effort to encourage them to go down. Sometimes it is said that the calves contrive to get upon the backs of the cows, and are conveyed in that way across the stream.

It not infrequently happens that the landing proves not to be good when the animals arrive on the further side, so that instead of a hard beach by which to ascend to the level of the plain, they find themselves sinking into quicksands or mire. The scene which is witnessed in a case like this presents sometimes, it is said, an aspect almost awful. The older and stronger beasts are perhaps able, after long-continued and desperate struggles, in which they trample down and climb over the others in their excitement and terror, to regain their footing and clamber up the bank; but often many are unable to extricate themselves, and perish miserably — their bodies being borne away by the current down the stream.

Crossing on the Ice

The case is still worse sometimes when the river is frozen, and the herd is consequently compelled to cross upon the ice. The animals have no means of judging of the strength of the ice except by taking the opinion of the leaders, who go down cautiously, and step in a timid, hesitating manner upon the margin of it, and then it if gives no sign of weakness under the weight of a single tread, they conclude it to be strong and proceed. But it may be strong enough to bear one, while far too weak to sustain the weight of a hundred.

Still the whole herd follow on, and perhaps when the head of the column has advance toward the middle of the stream, some cracking sound or other token of weakness gives the alarm. The leaders stop, the others press on, the ice becomes immensely overloaded, and presently goes down with a great crash, carrying hundreds into the water. Then ensues a scene of struggling and commotion and terror impossible to describe. Animals of every age and size are writhing and plunging in the water, vainly trying to climb up upon cakes of ice, or to force their way through the floating fragments to the shore — bellowing all the time with terror. Some at last gain the bank, but others are swept away in great numbers beneath the unbroken ice below and drowned.

Trails

In making their journeys the buffalos move in columns, those behind keeping in the track of those before, and in this way they make trails which soon become well worn; and being pretty wide, on account of the columns being formed with several animals abreast, they look like wagon roads. These roads extend, in some places, for hundreds of miles across the country. When they are once made they followed year after year by successive herds. In this respect the habits of the buffalo correspond with those of domestic cows in the pastures of New England, who lay out paths on the hill sides and in the woods, and continue to use them, when they are once worn, for many years.

Use of the Buffalo

The buffalo, as may readily be supposed, was a great resource to the Indians. His flesh furnished him with an abundant supply of excellent food. His skin served for cloth, and, when cut into thongs, for cords. His horns were made into vessels and implements of various kinds. Some tribes also made boats of his hide by stretching the hide, when green, over a frame made of a suitable form for the purpose intended. This, of course, was a very clumsy sort of craft, but being made without any seam, was perfectly water-tight and very serviceable.

The buffalo has many enemies, but the greatest of all is civilized man. So long as the vast herds were attacked only by bears, packs of wolves, and Indians armed simply with spears and arrows, they were able to hold their ground. The bulls of the herd, with their prodigious strength, and the formidable weapons with which natures has provided them in their horns, would maintain terrible conflicts with any of these foes, and would often come off victorious from the fight. but when the white man came, mounted upon a horse and armed with a rifle, no choice was left to him but to abandon the field; and in proportion as the tide of emigration moves onward toward the west, the buffalo retires before it, and will probably in time entirely disappear.

The frontiers, however, of his old dominion are drawn in very slowly and reluctantly, so that even the steamboat sometimes overtakes him. Cases have occurred in which steamboats, in feeling g their way up some of the western branches of the Mississippi and Missouri, have come upon a herd of buffalos crossing the stream, and the poor beasts, in the midst of their amazement at the spectacle, have been shot by the rifles of the passengers from the deck.

There is one case mentioned in which a steamboat passed so near a buffalo swimming in the water that a passenger on board, who had learned the use of the lasso in South America, threw a rope, with a slip noose at the end, through the air and caught him by the horns.

The crew then pulled the poor beast alongside of the steamer, and, getting slings under him, hoisted him on board and butchered him for his beef.

The Turkey

The turkey is one of the most valuable gifts made by the new world to the old. Until after the discovery of America no such animals was ever known in Europe, Asia, or Africa, though the forests and prairies of America were filled everywhere with flocks of these birds. The turkeys were accustomed to migrate to and fro from north to south, according as the food they lived upon was in season. In these journeys they marched on foot as long as they could keep the ground, only using their wings when there was a river to cross, or some other obstacle to be surmounted.

When they came to a river they used to pause long upon its bank before venturing to attempt the passage. They sometimes remained so for two or three days, during which time the old males would walk to and fro, strutting and gobbling with the greatest self importance, and with the air of being engaged in a deliberation of the utmost consequence to all the world.

At length, as it seemed, they would succeed in raising their courage to the proper point, and they would proceed to climb up to the topmost branches of the tallest trees growing near the river. There they would select their positions, and after a great deal more gobbling and strutting and innumerable false starts, they would commence their flight. The oldest and strongest birds would succeed in flying across the river before coming down to the ground, but the younger and feebler ones, especially if the river was wide, would fall into the water at a greater or less distance from the bank.

Then would follow a scene of floundering, scrambling and swimming, astonishing to behold, the result of which would be that the greater proportion of the flock would at last reach the land, though may of them would be carried by the force of the current far down the stream.

The value of the flesh of the turkey for food was soon made known to Europeans, and the bird is now domesticated, and has become very abundant, in almost every part of the world.

The Alligator

An alligator is an immense reptile of the lizard kind, which haunts the inlets, rivers, swamps and lagoons of the southern States in great numbers. When full grown it is a very terrible animal, on account of its great size and strength. It is sometimes fifteen or twenty feet long. it crawls slowly on the land, but it can move through the water with great speed. Its body is covered with horny scales, which form a coat of mail that is proof against a musket ball. It is only near the head and shoulders that the skin can be penetrated by even a rifle bullet.

Of course the alligator is a very formidable animal, the more so from his having an immense mouth, which is armed with rows of teeth of terrible aspect. Generally, however, he is pretty quiet in his disposition, and is often seen lying harmless, basking in the sun, on the shores of his lagoon, or crawling slowly along through the canes and flags that grow out of the slime. But sometimes, for example at certain seasons of the year, or when he is hungry, or has been in any way irritated or disturbed, he is very ferocious, and in such a case he becomes a dangerous as well as an ugly enemy.

The alligator, like most other reptiles, is very prolific. Indeed, one great function that the animal seems destined to fulfill in the economy of nature is that of producing eggs and rearing young, to be consumed as food by birds of prey. Only a small portion of its progeny survives the dangers which thus beset the period of their infancy.

The mothers make their nests in quite an artificial manner. They are built upon the ground, on the banks of lazy streams, or in the cane-brakes or marshes, and are of the form of great shallow cups, three or four feet in diameter. They are built of mud and grass, and a great many are usually constructed together, so as to form quite a village.

In these nests the northern alligator lays a great number of eggs, which she packs in mud, in several successive layers, one above the other, in the most singular manner. First she covers the floor of her nest with a sort of mortar which she spreads over it, made of mud and slime, and upon this lays one layer of eggs. This layer, when complete, she covers with another stratum of mortar, and over this lays another tier of eggs. The eggs have hard shells, and are somewhat larger than hen's eggs, and the monster lays so many of them as to build up her nest sometimes four or five feet high with these alternate layers.

When this work is finished the eggs are left to be hatched by the warmth of the sun, through the mother remains by them to guard them from the attacks of the pilferers that are always at hand in great numbers to steal and devour them. It has been said that in thus guarding these deposits the alligators in some sense make common cause, so that when one of the mothers has gone away to seek food, the others who remain watch over and protect her nest, and it is with some instinctive idea of this advantage that they adopt the plan of building their nests together.

There are sometimes not less than a hundred and fifty or two hundred eggs in a single nest. Of these, however, but a portion are hatched, and still fewer of the young arrive at maturity. The young that are hatched are watched and defended by their mothers with great care, but they are exceedingly tender and helpless, and great numbers of them are seized and devoured by beasts and birds of prey.

The greatest enemy of the alligator, however, is man. In gradually advancing the settlement of the countries in which they live, he intrudes more and more upon their haunts, and as their size is too great to allow them, like other reptiles, to secrete themselves from their pursuers, their numbers are all the time continually diminishing, and it is not improbable that before many years they may entirely disappear.

The crocodile of the Nile is an animal of the same general character with the alligator, but is of an altogether different species.

The Eagle

America is celebrated for its eagles. Indeed, one of the species, the bald eagle, so called, has been selected as the emblem of the national power. The eagles are all birds of prey, and they are remarkable for their size and the strength of their pinions. They seek their habitations on the summit of the various mountain ranges and on lofty cliffs overhanging the sea. From these elevated positions they survey vast regions of the air and watch for their prey. For this purpose they are endowed with powers of vision of almost incredible acuteness.

The eagle has always been held in high estimation by the American Indians, and his plumage has been prized more than that of any other bird for the dress and the decorations of warriors. This high estimation is derived partly from the warlike courage and propensities of the bird itself, and partly probably from the difficulty of taking him. Thus, eagles' feathers attached to a head-dress of a native chief, or ornamenting the shaft of a spear, were not only emblems of courage and strength proper to signalize the martial spirit of the wearer as a warrior, but they were also trophies of the daring and skill which he displayed as a huntsman, in scaling the lofty heights where alone they were to be procured.

The eagle is very long-lived. Some specimens have been known to live from eighty to a hundred years.

cochineal

The forests of America produce a great many different woods which have been used extensively in dyeing, and for other similar purposes in the arts, but the most important pigment that has been derived from the productions of this country is cochineal.

The cochineal is an insect. It is of the form of a little bug. It is a native of Mexico. It feeds upon certain species of cactus. Immense numbers of these plants are cultivated in Mexico and Peru, for the sake of the insects that feed upon them. The work of collecting these insects, which is very slow and tedious, is performed by women, who go about among the cactus plants and brush the bugs off into a basket with a little brush made of the tail of a squirrel, or of some other animal.

The insects, when collected, are killed by being thrown into boiling water, and then are carefully dried by being placed in ovens, or exposed to the sun. The article is then ready for market.

The cochineal insect produces a beautiful crimson dye, though a scarlet color can be obtained from it by a certain mode of using it. It is an article of very great value. Several millions of dollars' worth are annually exported from South America, and it is so precious that it is regarded in the markets of the world almost in the light of gold. Indeed it sometimes fulfills the functions of gold by being used for remittances and for making payments.

The Rattlesnake and Humming Bird

There are two other animals that remain to be mentioned among those that are peculiar to America — animals that, however dissimilar in other respects, are alike in this, namely, that each is marked by a very striking peculiarity of the same general kind, while nothing at all approaching to either exists in any other part of the known world. These two animals are the rattlesnake and the humming-bird. The peculiarity which gives them special distinction is a power of producing a sound by the motion of a part of their bodies — the humming bird by its wings and the rattlesnake by its tail.

The Rattle

The tail of the rattle snake is provided with several joints, formed of a bony substance, and put together in a loose manner, so that when shaken they produce a rattling sound. Whether the design of nature in giving the snake this instrument is to enable it to warn other animals and men of the danger of coming too near, or for some other purpose, we can only conjecture.

There is a mystery, too, in respect to its venom. Some have supposed that this venom was given to it as a means of killing its prey before devouring it. Other serpents are endowed with the power of killing their prey by the prodigious force which they can exercise in coiling round the limbs of the animal they have seized, breaking its bones in the terrible gripe which they give it, and thus putting a sudden and total stop to all the vital operations. All serpents seem to require some extraordinary means of killing their prey, for they are formed to live upon animals much larger than themselves, and which they could not kill by any ordinary means.

There is a considerable number of species of serpents with rattling tails in America, but it is singular that there are none of any kind in the old world. The whole tribe of rattlesnakes is an American production altogether.

The Rattlesnake more Sinned Against Than Sinning

Notwithstanding the hatred with which the rattlesnake is regarded and the opprobrium which is cast upon him by man, he seems, after all, to be more sinned against than sinning, for he really is a very quiet and peaceable beast, that has no quarrel with man, and never injures him unless he honestly supposes that he is called to do it in self-defense. If he sees a man coming toward him, he crawls quietly away, if a way of retreat is open to him, If not, and if his enemy still approaches with an aggressive air, he feels himself justified in defending himself by the only means with which nature has provided him. He winds himself up into a spiral coil, with his head projecting from the center of it, and as soon as his enemy comes near, he darts forward and upward, and strikes his fang into his enemy's flesh, at a point as high from the ground as he can attain.

He Acts Always on the Defensive

He, however, seldom or never attacks man of his own accord, but warns him away by sounding his rattle when he sees him coming inadvertently near. It results from this his peaceable disposition that, though the prairies in the western country, and the forests at the south, are full of rattlesnakes, numbering probably millions upon millions, and the slaves upon the plantations, and the farmers and emigrants and railway laborers in the woods, are continually encountering them, it is very rare that lives are lost from their venom. How great must be the forbearance, we might almost say the generosity exercised by the reptile, to lead to such a result as this!

This generosity, however, if generosity it be, seems to be very little appreciated by man. Man everywhere attacks and kills every rattlesnake that he sees. He strikes him on the neck with a club if he wishes to kill him at a blow; and if, on the other hand, which is more frequently the case, he wishes to tease and torment him for a while before putting him to death, or if he wishes to capture him, he comes with a forked stick, and sets the prongs of it into the ground, one on each side of the poor victim's neck. He then grasps his neck behind the stick with his hand and takes him up with impunity. It is even possible, while holding him thus, to extract his fang, or the little bag of poison at the root of it, and thus render him entirely harmless.

The Humming Bird

From the rattlesnake, one of the most repulsive of all animals to man, we turn with pleasure to the humming bird, an animal that likewise owes a part of his celebrity to a sound that he makes, though the instrument with which he makes it is a pair of wings instead of a tail. Whatever of mystery there may be about the rattling made by the reptile, there is none in respect to the humming noise made by the bird. The sound is due simply to the rapidity of the vibrations of the wings, and this is due to the smallness of the bird. For the smaller the bird and the smaller the wings, the more rapid must be the motion of them to sustain the weight of the body in the air.

Vibrations Producing Sound

Sound is produced by the vibration of any substance in contact with the air, by which vibrations are imparted to the air, and thus transmitted to the ear. If the vibrations are slow no audible sound is produced. Thus the motion of the pendulum of a clock, the wagging of the tail of a dog, the motion of the hand up and down in the air, as rapid as it is possible to make such a motion, produce no sound.

As we increase the rapidity of such vibrations, however, we at last come to a limit where a sound begins to be heard. This is about thirty-two beats in a second. The humming bird's wings, therefore, must move to and fro more than thirty-two beats in a second, and it is simply in consequence of the fact that his body and wings are so small that the rapidity of the motion of his wings comes within the limit above referred to, and sound is produced. The wings of a swallow make less than thirty-two pulsations in a second, and thus that bird moves through the air silently.

As the rapidity of the vibrations of any moving body increases the sound becomes higher in pitch. Thus the wings of a mosquito, moving much more rapidly than those of a humming bird, made a more acute sound. As the rapidity increase still more, we reach at last a point where sound is no longer produced. This limit varies with different ears, but with most persons it is at about eight thousand vibrations a second that sound ceases to be heard. This upper limit, however, is extremely vague.

The number of vibrations corresponding with the middle c of a musical instrument, according to the diapason recently established by the French government, if five hundred and twenty-two. That of a sound one octave below is half as great; of one an octave above is twice as great. Thus by finding the pitch of the sound made by the wings of a humming bird, by means of a piano forte or other instrument, the number of vibrations made by them in a second can be approximately ascertained.

The Humming Bird's Mode of Life

The humming bird is designed, like the bee, to feed on the sweet juices found in flowers. But being a bird, and thus, small as he is, too large and heavy to alight upon the flower and rest his weight upon it, he is provided with wings to poise himself in the air, and a long slender bill to serve as a pipe with which to draw out the juices from the innermost recesses of the largest corollas.

There are a great many different species of humming birds, all peculiar to America. None are found in any part of the old world. There is a difference in the form, and also in the plumage of the different species. In some of them the feathers, especially those of the neck and breast, are splendidly iridescent, glowing with all the colors of the richest gems. Nothing can exceed the beautiful effect of these colors when the bird is seen poised in the sun before the flower from which he is extracting the juices with his long and slender bill. At such a time his wings cannot be seen, so swift is their motion; or if a glimpse of them is obtained, they produce only the effect of a little quivering mist at his sides. He seems like a wingless bird poised motionless in mid air.

If at such a time anything occurs to alarm him or to attract his attention, he darts off through the air a little way, quick as a flash, then suddenly stopping and poising himself upon his wings, he rests as motionless as if he were standing upon the ground. Then, after contemplating for a moment the object that alarmed him, he shoots off again through the air, with a motion so quick that the eye can scarcely follow him — and is gone.

Sometimes artificial flowers are made of the feathers of the humming bird, especially those taken from the breast — the different colors being arranged to represent the different parts of the flower. Nothing can exceed the gorgeous beauty of these imitation.

Gentleness of Disposition

Humming birds are of a very gentle disposition, and they could be easily tamed were it not that they are of too delicate a constitution to bear confinement; and thus, whenever they are brought into the house and shut up in a cage or an aviary, they soon droop and die. While they are thus kept they must be fed with fresh flowers, or else with honey, thinned with a little water.

They build their nests upon shrubs or upon the stems of vines or other climbing plants, nor far from the ground, and the nests are so small that, when seen from a short distance, one of them might very easily be mistaken for a little tuft of moss, or a moss-covered knot upon the wood. There are two eggs only laid in the nest. They are white, and not much larger than peas.

These birds are very common in the West Indies and in all the tropical parts of America. A young English gentleman, who was about embarking for England, happened, just before he went on board his ship, to find a humming bird's nest with the mother sitting upon it, sitting. He approached very gently to the place. The bird watched him anxiously, but she was too intent upon her duty to her eggs to fly away. The gentleman carefully cut off the branch and carried, it, nest, bird, and all, on board the ship, intending to present his prize to a lady of his acquaintance on reaching his native land.

He fed the bird on home and water during the voyage. She became quite tame, and continued on the nest until the little birds were hatched, but before the end of the voyage she died.

The little birds lived to reach the land. The gentleman presented them to the lady for whom the present was intended. One of them died very soon, but the other lived a month or two, and was so tame that he would put his bill to his mistress's lips and draw out honey and water from a little supply which she had provided for him there. It was to him just as if her lips had been the petal of a flower.

THE INDIAN RACES

Question of the Origin of the Different Races of Men

Whether it would seem more probable, judging by the light afforded us by the observation of nature alone, and without regard to the declarations of Scripture, that all the different races of men have descended from one common stock, or that each race had a different origin, and thus now forms a different species from the rest, is a question that has been much discussed by naturalists and philosophers.

In making these inquiries several considerations have operated upon the minds of philosophers to lead them to set out of the case the testimony of the Scriptures. In the first place, some of the most distinguished naturalists and philosophers do not believe in the divine authority of the Scriptures, but regard them simply as ancient writings, of great moral and historical value indeed, but yet not at all of infallible authority on any subject. Others, who believe in the Scriptures as a revelation of the divine will, think that they are intended to guide us only in matters of faith and practice, and that it was not the design of the Holy Spirit, in indicting them, to teach us science and philosophy, but to leave us, in respect to those branches of knowledge, entirely to our own observations and studies in the field of nature itself.

There is a third class still, namely, those who think that while every inference which may be fairly drawn, even from the incidental allusions contained in the Scriptures, may be entirely relied upon as a truth revealed to us by divine authority, whatever may be the subject to which it relates, we are not to take these inferences with us, either to aid or restrict us, when we go forth into the field of the world as students of natures, but are to act independently, and avail ourselves of the lights of science and philosophy alone. They think, in other words, that the true object which we should have in view in studying nature is simply to learn what nature herself teaches, and that in doing this we must interpret what we see solely by the light of our reason and reflection. We may distrust the conclusions that we come to, when we arrive at them, if we find that they conflict with convictions obtained in other ways, but in the process of coming to these conclusions we must be guided honestly and entirely by what our observations of nature herself teaches, and by those alone.

Distinction of Races

There are four or five and perhaps many more distinct races of men upon the earth, each separated from the rest by very decided and apparently very permanent lines of demarcation. The differences are not merely those of color, or of any other external mark, but they relate quite as much to the internal organization of the individual, both bodily and mental. These different races are subdivided into many others, all marked by distinctive lines, more or less decisive and permanent. The great question for naturalists to solve has been whether, judging from the light of science alone, without any aid from the declarations of Scripture, we should conclude that all these different forms have descended from one pair.

Now, although, in coming to their conclusion on this subject, philosophers have set the authority of the Scriptures, for the time being, aside, it is remarkable that the conclusion which they have come to corresponds with and confirms the testimony of the Mosaic records; for the whole body of naturalists, with few if any exceptions, have concurred in the opinion that the differences between the various races of men, great as they are, and permanent as they seem to be within the periods subject to our observation, are not specific differences — that is, that they are not such as, judging from observations made in other divisions of the animal world, imply a separate original parentage. In other words, that there is nothing in them which should preclude the idea of their all being descended from a single pair.

Causes of the Differences Observed

It has been very common to presume, on the supposition that all the races of men were descended from a single pair, that the only causes which can account for the diversities of race which we now observe consist in differences of climate, of food, of modes of life, and of other such external influences as these. And some persons, after attempting to prove that such causes as these are not sufficient to account for changes so great, have inferred that all the races could not have descended from the same pair.

But there is another class of causes of a totally different nature from these, and far more powerful, which have undoubtedly operated very extensively in producing these changes. The existence of them is well known, though the nature and operation of them is very imperfectly understood.

These causes are the hidden influences which produce those mental or bodily peculiarities which are born with us, in contradistinction from those which are subsequently produced by education, the circumstances of life, or external influences. A child whose skin is browned or darkened by playing in the sun is an example of one species of effect. A child born with a dark complexion is an example of the other kind.

The kinds of difference between parents and off spring of this innate character are very numerous, and sometimes very striking. A gentle and amiable father and mother may give birth to a very forward and irritable child. It is often the case, it is true, that such forwardness and irritability may be the result of bad management, but still there are cases where it is impossible to doubt that they have their origin in the inner constitution of the body or of the mind. In the same manner, parents who both have black hair and black eyes may give birth to a child with blue eyes and auburn hair.

We see the same differences spontaneously arising from births in the animal creation. There are black cats and grey cats, and tawny cats and white cats, and yet nobody supposes that these difference are produced by differences of climate, or by any other external cause whatever.

Important Conclusion

We conclude from this that even if it were proved that differences of climate and other similar causes are not sufficient to account for the great diversities which prevail among the different races of men, it is very far from being proved, on that account, that these several races must each have had an independent origin. There are other causes, far more deeply seated and more radical and powerful in their action, which may have operated in addition to these, and perhaps in combination with them, to produce the results.

The Distinction of Race Fixed and Permanent

The differences which we observe in comparing the different races of men with one another, although we grant that they have resulted either from the operation of secret internal or of known external causes, or both, taking effect upon one single species which descended from one single pair, are still very great, and they are fixed and permanent. By this it is not meant that they are absolutely and perpetually permanent, for it is obvious that the operation of the same causes which produced them may remove or reverse them, but only that they are permanent through any moderate number of successive generations, and not removable by means of any outward influences which man can bring to bear upon them. In other words, as they have not probably been produced by the operation of external causes which are under the control of men, so they cannot be removed by such causes.

The operation of outward influences, such as those of education and mode of life, will produce great effects; but such causes do not change the real and essential characteristics of the race. The Indian remains an Indian, and the African an African, under all the changes of circumstances to which he can be subjected, and in a vast majority of cases he approximates toward the characteristics of the Caucasian race only so far as Caucasian blood flows in his veins.

Objection To This View

Some persons are very reluctant to admit that any race of men is marked by a fixed and permanent characteristic of inferiority to the others, for fear that this will be made an excuse by unjust and wicked men for treating them oppressively and cruelly; but there surely can be no justification for tyranny in the weakness and helplessness of the object of it. To believe that people of the Indian race, for example, are inferior in intellectual capacity and power to those of European descent, is no reason for believing that it is right to defraud and oppress them by depriving them of their lands or other property without a fair equivalent, or being guilty of any wrong or injustice toward them whatever.

The Weak Especially Entitled to Protection From the Strong

Indeed, the contrary of this is true. The weak and the helpless in any community, instead of being rightfully subject to the oppression of the strong, are specially entitled to protection. If the Author of nature, in order to provide for the more efficient and easy performance of some of the subordinate functions of society to which a high state of civilization gives rise, or for the occupation of certain portions of the earth not adapted to a high state of civilization, or which are from any cause temporarily precluded from it, has prepared races of men with faculties and sentiments which adapt them to this work or to those situations — faculties and sentiments which fit them to be the employed rather than the employers, to labor rather than to plan, to endure fatigue rather than assume and bear responsibility — surely all generous minds among the higher races will see in that relation a reason, not for taking advantage of their power to do injustice to those thus placed at their mercy, but rather to use it for their protection. They will feel bound, when engaging in any common operation, as, for example, in employing them to hunt and trap for furs among the lakes and forests of the north country, to take care that while they themselves plan and superintend, and their less capable auxiliaries labor and toil to execute, the anvils of the common industry shall be so divided as to give to their subordinates the fair and proper share, whatever that may be, for the part which they perform. In this way, though themselves in no respect equal to the higher races, they may enjoy equal rights with them, namely, the same protection and the same enjoyment of the fair and proper reward, comparatively small though it be, for the performance of the inferior functions which their capacity enables them to fulfill.

There is no need, therefore, of maintaining that the Indian is equal to the Caucasian, in order to prevent our having an excuse for oppressing and abusing him. The more inferior and the more helpless he is, the greater is his claim on the higher and nobler race for justice and protection.

Original Peopling of the Continent

On the supposition that the American continent was originally peopled by a branch or branches of the human family migrating from the old world, there have been a great many speculations in respect to the time and the manner of their first introduction.

In the first place, they may have come from the northern part of Europe, by the way of Norway and Iceland, to Greenland, and thence down through Labrador to the lake country, and thus have spread through the whole interior of the continent.

The supposition that they may have come in this way, or at least that some may have so come, is confirmed by the fact that there is a great resemblance between some of the Indian tribes and the Scandinavian nations, so called, who inhabit the northern parts of Europe and Asia.

Crossing the Northern Seas

In respect to the manner in which these supposed emigrants crossed the seas in coming from the north of Europe on one side, or the north of Asia on the other — for the water which separates the new continent from the old is still narrower on the western side than it is on the eastern — several suppositions may be made. They may have been blown off from their own shores by accident. The people in all those regions live a great deal upon the sea. They make boats of a very substantial character, and evince a great deal of skill and courage in navigating them. In fact, they are compelled to acquire great skill and to exercise great courage in these pursuits, for they obtain almost all their living on the ice-floes, or upon the water between them, and thus they are in constant danger of being caught in the ice and carried away. These ice-floes are kept by the winds and currents in a state of constant motion, and are carried by them hundreds of miles over the sea, and a party caught upon one of them might, perhaps, by making a hut of their boat and killing seals and white bears and other animals that frequent them for food, succeed in making quite a long voyage on such an embarkation in safety.

Traveling Upon the Ice

Then, again, a whole tribe or congeries of families might undertake to migrate purposely over the ice, to escape from enemies or from famine. They might travel very far on such expeditions, over ice either fixed or moving, with sledges drawn by dogs or reindeer. The Laplanders and the Esquimaux, it is found at the present day, make very long journeys in this way.

The Pacific Islanders

Scattered over almost all parts of the Pacific Ocean are groups of islands which are inhabited by races of men that are almost as much at home on the sea as upon the shore. A boat for the water is sometimes an object of even greater necessity to them than a hut for the land; and the magnitude of some of the boats which the islanders that are most advanced in these arts are able to construct and navigate is truly wonderful

Indeed, these islanders, like the inhabitants of the Arctic regions, have every possible inducement to become seamen, and they enjoy every facility for learning and practicing the nautical art. In the first place, there is no possible communication between the different islands of the same group except by water. Then, moreover, between the different parts of the same island the passage is made much more easily by sea than by land, for the water near the shore is almost always smooth, being protected by coral reefs coming up to the surface at a short distance from the land, while the way through the interior is obstructed by almost impassible thickets, or is made rough and impracticable by volcanic rocks, which the savages have no means of leveling or removing.

It results from this state or things that these islanders all acquire a great degree of skill in navigating the seas around them. The children take to the water at the earliest age. They find it always warm, and, as they wear no clothing, it is difficult to say which they love best — playing in the surf upon the water, or in the sun upon the shore.

The children begin their attempts at navigation by means of any floating substance that they can lay their hands upon, almost as soon as they can walk. Shipmasters, who touch at these islands to get fresh provisions for their crews, say that they have known children not more than three years old to swim out to the ship anchored in the offing, having only a cocoa nut, with the husk left on, to buoy themselves up with in the water.

In some of the islands the native build canoes of great size and of very complicated construction, and capable, some of them, of conveying a considerable supply of provisions. With these they undertake quite extended expeditions, either of war, of commerce, or of migration. Such boats as these must often be driven away from their course, and carried by winds and currents to distant lands. It is undoubtedly in this way that the innumerable islands of the Pacific Ocean have become stocked, and it is not at all improbable that similar migrations may have taken place in former ages to the American shores.

Currents of the Ocean

This supposition is rendered still more probable from the fact that it is now ascertained that the ocean is subject to the flow of certain great permanent currents, which have the velocity and the force and the steady continuance of the currents of rivers, only on a much grander scale than any rivers in the world. A large canoe driven out of its course, and containing a good supply of provisions, might be carried a very long distance on one of these ocean streams, even without any assistance from the wind.

Antiquity of the Aboriginal Population of America,

The remoteness of the period in which the progenitors of the Indian tribes came to America is shown by the number of distinct Indian language which have been formed, and by the great dissimilarity which exists between these languages and any now known in other parts of the world.

A language once formed, even though unwritten, is extremely permanent. It is subject to slight modifications and changes, it is true, such as those by which different dialects are formed in different provinces of the same country; but to make a radical change in the form and structure of a language requires a very long course of time. Now, the languages of America are essentially different, not only in the words but in the whole system on which they are founded, from any languages of the old world, and they are also divided into several distinct classes, which are almost totally different from each other.

This shows that the process of bringing the American languages to their present state has been going on for a very long time and, consequently, that the separation of the races speaking them from the original stock in the old world must have taken place at a very remote period.

Ancient Nations of North America

At the time when America was discovered nations were found in the central and southern part of the continent that had attained to quite a high degree of civilization, and many ruins of ancient temples and cities are now from time to time discovered in those countries overgrown with enormous trees, the roots of which are intertwined with the remains of other enormous trees, which show that the structures that they cover must have been in ruins for a great many centuries.

There are no such ruins of ancient cities in the territory now belonging to the United States, but there are remains of ancient fortifications and mounds, of an extremely curious character, scattered through very extensive regions of the western country, which indicate the existence there in former times of a higher civilization and different modes of life from those manifested by the present race of Indians.

Durability of Earthworks

It is a very singular fact that works formed of earth and grassed over are among the most permanent and lasting of all the constructions made by man. The grassy mounds in the country of Nineveh and Babylon have remained without the least apparent change for many centuries. There are also in England old druidical mounds, and rings in the grass called fairy rings, which have been known and described in books from the earliest periods of English history, and they remain now, from century to century, apparently without any change, while hundreds of massive buildings of stone have gone entirely to decay, and the ruins of those that still remain are found to change rapidly, if neglected, from year to year. In the first settled portions of the United States, too, it is not improbable that the oldest structures of which any traces now remain are the beaver dams.

In fact, any artificial conformation of the surface of the ground, once well covered with greensward, and left undisturbed by the plough, seems to be more enduring than any other work of man.

The remains of ancient fortifications in the upper part of the valley of the Mississippi are very numerous, and they are on a very extended scale. They are laid out regularly, and denote the existence of considerable towns, or of places of encampments for large bodies of men. In some of them spaces of fifty and a hundred acres are inclosed.

Ancient Fields

There are also in certain parts of the prairies marks of ancient corn fields, of every great size, and extending over the country for a hundred and fifty miles. The land in these fields lies in ridges, like those always seen in a corn field that is left, after the corn is harvested, to grass itself over, without being leveled by the plough and harrow. These ridges are so regular, and they are confined so strictly to circumscribed and well defined fields — fields, too, occupying situations exactly suitable for the cultivation of corn — as to leave no room for doubt in respect to the nature of them.

They are very ancient too, as is proved by the trees often found standing upon them. Some persons, in examining these fields, once caused an oak tree to be cut down which was growing in one of them, and on counting the layers of wood they found that the tree was three hundred and twenty-five years old. This carries the time when the fields were cultivated far beyond the settlement of the country by Europeans; and inasmuch as no Indian tribes have been known, since the coming of Europeans; to cultivate the ground so extensively, it is supposed that these fields denote that in ancient times there existed a more numerous and civilized population over all this region than exists at the present day.

The Copper Mines

This opinion is confirmed by certain indications that are observed in the Lake Superior copper region. Ancient mines are found here with traces of former workings that are on a scale fare beyond the capacity of the Indians of the present day.

Copper is a metal that comes into use in the history of civilization much earlier than iron, for copper is often found in a metallic and malleable condition, in its native state, while iron, being so easily oxidizable, almost always exists in the form of an ore, which it is necessary to reduce by a highly artificial process before the iron can be obtained. To make implements of copper it is only necessary to find masses of native metal of the proper size, such as are often found upon or near the surface of the ground, and then to bring them to the required shape by hammering them with smooth and hard stones, or by grinding them upon rough ones.

Accordingly, as might naturally be expected, copper implements and ornaments have been, from time immemorial, very much in use among all the Indian tribes. But at the period of the discovery of America, and since that time, the supply of copper for these purposes was obtained almost entirely from specimens found near the surface of the ground. There is no evidence of any systematic or extended workings of the mines within a period of several centuries; but there is abundant evidence that before that time, as is shown by the age of the trees growing over the old excavations, mining operations in this region were carried on upon a very considerable scale. The miners of the present day frequently come to old trenches, half filled in and grassed over, and with immense trees growing in them, at the bottom of which, when they dig them out anew, they find remains of the ancient works. They come down, when digging in such places, to great masses of copper blocked up on skids of wood which have been preserved from decay by lying all the time in water, with marks of fire upon them, and broken tools lying all around.

The tools which these old miners used were very curious. The principal one was a sort of hammer made of a smooth and hard stone. The handle of these hammers, instead of passing through the stone, was formed of a withe, and was carried round it in a small groove, which they contrived in some way to pick in the stone. The withe was brought round the stone in this groove while it was green, and the two ends were then twisted together and secured by a cord wound round tight, close to the stone. Then when the withe became dry it formed a very stiff and substantial handle, and the groove prevented it from slipping off the stone.

Trees have been found growing over ancient works in these mines with five hundred concentric layers of wood in them, proving that the excavations and the works carried on in them were finally abandoned at least five hundred years ago.

The Mounds of Florida

Mounds of a somewhat similar character to those existing in the western country are found in Florida, many of which contain human bones in considerable quantities, indicating that they were used as places of sepulture. In one the bones of a very large person were found placed in a horizontal position in the center, and around it, in a circle, the skeletons of a number of other persons — these last being in a sitting position.

In another mound there were two layers of skeletons, one above the other. In both layers the bodies were arranged in a circle, with the heads toward the center and the feet toward the circumference of the mound.

In most of these mounds fragments of pottery were found. These relics consist of pieces of broken jars, kettles, stew-pans, porringers, and other domestic utensils of that sort. In many cases the vessels were whole, with the exception of a small hole in the bottom of each, which appeared to have been purposely made. This may have been done to render the utensils useless, in order that there might be no inducement to tempt any persons to violate the graves with the intent of robbing them of articles buried with the deceased owners.

Some of these specimens gave indications of considerable art in the manufacture of them, being ornamented with various devices worked in the clay. One had a hollow handle, which was so fashioned, in connection with the cavity of the vessel itself, as to indicate that it was meant to be used as a sort of funnel to pour out the liquid into smaller vessels without spilling it.

Whether these articles had been baked in the fire or sun-dried it was found difficult to ascertain; as also it was to determine whether they were fashioned by the and or upon a potter's wheel. The making of vessels out of clay by the hand is one of the very first steps taken by all savages in their attempts at art. Learning to indurate them, by baking them in the fire, is the second step; and making a wheel to fashion them upon, by putting the mass of clay in revolution in order to facilitate giving it a true circular form, is a third step, and one much in advance of the other two.

The remains of a potter's wheel, with a mass of clay upon it partly fashioned into a vessel, was found some years since in a mound in Georgia, and this at first seemed to afford positive proof that the Indians understood the art of shaping their pottery by means of a revolution of the clay. It was, however, afterward though not impossible that this wheel might have been introduced by the Spaniards, who very early made incursions into that part of the country and attempted to found settlements there. Indeed, the Spaniards were so early in their visits to the shores of the Gulf of Mexico, and the French to those of the great lakes, that considerable care is necessary to avoid attributing to the aboriginal Indians relics and indications which were really left by their European visitors.

Unquestionable Antiquity of Many of the Mounds

Although many of the mounds now found may be of comparatively modern date, there are some which, like those on the Ohio and the other western rivers, bear incontestable evidence of great antiquity in the immense trees that are found growing upon them. There are live-oaks standing upon some of these tumuli of such size that they are estimated to be six or seven hundred years old. This would carry back the date of the mound to a period two or three centuries anterior to the time of Columbus.

In many instances, on the other hand, the mounds are situated in open plains, or are covered with thickets consisting of plants and trees of moderate age. In such cases as these it is difficult to determine the question of the antiquity of the mound, except so far as a reasonable judgment may be formed from the character and appearance of the objects found within it.

Conclusion

On the whole, there is abundant evidence in these ancient remains that this continent has been inhabited by the ancestors of the present Indian races for a very long period. It is, moreover, generally supposed that in former times the population was far more numerous, and that the nations composing it were far more advanced in civilization than those found in possession of the country when the Europeans first visited these shores.

THE INDIAN FAMILY

The Institution of Marriage

The Indians, as all other communities of human beings in every age, in every clime, and in every possible condition in respect to civilization or barbarism, have done, lived in families — the husband, the wife, and the children forming a natural group and dwelling together in common, the children remaining under the care of themselves; and the husband and wife, once joined, remaining united for life.

Some persons have imagined that the institution of marriage is an artificial institution, adopted by society as an arrangement proved by experiment to be, on the whole, most advantageous to man. But the universality of this institution proves that it is of higher origin. it is a part of man's nature, considered as an animal, that he should have one female partner, and that the union which binds him to his partner, when once she is chosen, should endure for life.

It is curious to observe that the provision of nature by which man is led everywhere, and under all circumstances, to the institution of marriage as the foundation of the social state, is in accordance with a general principle which pervades the whole animal creation. The principle is this:

General Law of Pairing

In all cases where the nurture of the young of any animal, for any reason, requires more than the mother herself alone can do for them, it seems to be a general law of nature in respect to such animals that they are provided with instincts which lead them to pair. A male and female unite, and they remain united until the young no longer need their joint assistance.

Thus birds pair, because it is necessary that both should co-operate to build the nest, and also that the father should bring food while the mother sits upon the eggs to hatch them. And lions pair, for one must remain and take care of the young, while the other goes away on distant excursions to procure food.

But sheep and other such animals do not pair, for their young do not require the joint attention of father and mother.

In respect to the duration of the union thus formed, the principle is that it continues as long as the necessity for it continues; that is, as long as the brood of young ones require the united efforts of both father and mother to protect them. Then — at least so it is supposed in the case of birds — when the season is over and the young ones are grown up to maturity, the union is terminated, the pair separate, and each, at the commencement of a new season, chooses a mate again.

Application to the Case of Man

Now, in the case of man, the young require the aid of both parents for their nurture and protection; and inasmuch as each requires this attention for ten or twelve years at least, and as during the time while the first-born is attaining this age others succeed, the period during which the con-join effort of the parents are required is protracted, without intermission, during the whole of their lives — that is, through all the portion of it during which their natural vigor continues unimpaired. It follows from this, and from the fact that the numbers of the sexes are equal, that according to the analogy of nature we should have expected that the human species would be provided with instincts leading them to unite in pairs, and to continue so united for life.

We find, accordingly, that this is the fact everywhere. The marriage laws of all human societies are consequently made to guard and protect the marriage institution — not to establish it. The institution itself is founded in instincts and principles of our nature existing antecedent to all law.

Indeed, the family institution, instead of waiting to be established by law, is often even more important and more prominent in low states of civilization than in high. It is most powerful where laws are weakest. Instead of being created by law and thus following it in the order or time, it is itself rather the origin and source of law. So far as we have any opportunity to trace back the forms of social organization to their source, we find them arising usually, in the first instance, from that primordial and elementary bond, the union of husband with wife, which springs at once from the physical constitution and innate instincts of man, and is the germ from which all other systems of authority and subordination come.

It was eminently so among the Indians. They lived in families throughout the length and breadth of the land — the families of the same connection being grouped together in tribes. They lived generally in peace, and were engaged in labors of patient industry for providing food and clothing for themselves and their children.

Construction of Dwellings

The dwellings of the Indians were generally made of poles covered with bark or mats. The ends of the poles were set in the ground in a ring of holes made to receive them, and then the tops were tied together in a point above, so as to give the hut a conical form. Sometimes, however, the ring was made larger, and then the ends of the poles were lapped upon each other, each opposite pair being joined in this way. By this mode of fashioning the frame the hut would receive a hemispherical form — that is, the form of a dome — a structure much less convenient than the other.

In other cases the poles would be set in two long rows of holes, made at a suitable distance from each other, and each opposite pair would then be lapped together and tied. Poles were then laid lengthwise along the roof thus formed and tied at the crossings. These lengthwise poles acted as stays to give strength and stiffness to the frame. When the frame was thus completed it was covered with mats or bark. Of course, a hut made in this way would be of a semi-cylindrical form, like a long arbor built over a walk in a garden. Some lodges made in this way were intended to accommodate many families, and were very large.

Coverings

The bark used for the covering of the huts and lodges was commonly birch bark, a kind which peels off the tree in large thin sheets, and is of a substance, too, which is completely impervious to water. These sheets of bark could be rolled up in a very compact form, as matting or carpeting is rolled with us.

These strips peel off in a direction round the tree, and of course cannot be longer than the circumference of the tree from which they are taken. But a tree of two feet and a half in diameter, not an unusual size in the native forests of the country; would yield strips seven and eight feet long, which would be amply sufficient for the purpose intended, They were usually taken off the tree in pieces from two to three feet wide.

In putting on these sheets the upper end was fastened to the upper part of the frame — leaving a space open for chimney — and the lower end came down to the ground. A round stick was rolled a little way into this lower end and sewed in. This stick helped to strengthen the end, and also assisted in holding it in its place. A stone was laid upon it when necessary, to keep it down. It also served as a roller to roll the sheet upon when the family removed; for these sheets of bark, once prepared, were considered quite valuable, and they were always taken away in cases of removal, though the poles which formed the frame were often left behind.

In some cases tribes living in the western country, on the banks of the Upper Missouri, where perhaps birch bark could not be obtained, covered the frames of their wigwams with flat stones set up against the poles, in such a way that they leaned in some measure upon them. These stones were arranged around the frame, tier above tier, each tier resting upon he edges of the tier below, and leaning against the frame. The joints were plastered with a mortar made of clay.

Of course, for such a covering as this it was necessary to make the frame very much stronger than when a lighter one was to be used.

Interior of the Lodges

The large lodges often contained several families, each of whom occupied its own particular portion of the interior. In such cases the different tenants were very careful not to encroach upon each other's domains. There was a fire in the middle of the lodge, and mats and skins for the members of the different families were laid down upon the ground in different situations around it. The sleeping places were back under the roof, the beds being also make of mats and skins.

When there were babies, beds were made for them of the finest moss, with a skin spread over it that was covered with some soft fur.

It was the pride of the mistress of this strange household to keep everything in good order in her domain. She maintained a bright and cheerful fire in the fire-place when the weather was cold, and kept the ground nicely swept and clean all around it. Then when all was arranged she would take her place upon her own mat or skin, and employ herself in sewing a roller into a new sheet of bark, or in making mats, or moccasins, or snowshoes, while her husband, in his place near by, was employed in fashioning spears or arrows, or in making other hunting or fishing gear, and the children sat musing silently by the fire, or tumbled over each other in their play, upon a bear-skin in the corner.

Indian Housekeeping

Among the Indians the whole charge of the housekeeping

devolved upon the women, as with us, but in their understanding of this term much more was included than in ours. It comprised building the house as well as taking care of it, and also the making of all the furniture. It was the work of the women to cut the poles and set them in the ground, to have always on hand a good supply of bark to cover the frame, and to take the work apart and put it together again, in case of removal. They had also to cultivate the corn fields, store the grain when it was collected, and prepare the food.

Removals

Although each tribe continued in most cases to occupy the same territory from generation to generation, still removals from place to place within the territory were very common. The best places for cultivating corn, and for fishing in the summer season, were not usually the best for hunting and trapping the wild animals of the woods in the winter. Accordingly there were frequent occasions to remove a family or a settlement from place to place; and in order to facilitate these migrations the wigwams were almost always built on the borders of streams, so that the sheets of bark for roofs, the mats, the skins, the cooking utensils, and the other household goods, might be conveyed to the new locality by water in canoes.

Canoes

These canoes themselves were made of birch bark, There was first a frame made of strips of wood of about the size and thickness of a common kitchen-basket handle, and then the whole was covered with sheets of bark, very neatly and strongly sewed. The thread for such sewing was made of the fibers of certain kinds of bark twisted into filaments by rubbing them with a rolling motion on the knee, or of thongs cut from the hides of animals. It was wonderful to see with what skill the Indian women would execute this sewing, so as to make a firm, compact and substantial seam, and without leaving any perceptible openings at the stitches. The boat would be almost watertight when it was first put together, and it was soon made perfectly so by paying over the seams with pitch obtained from some species of the pine, or other resin-bearing tree.

The upper edge of the boat all around was strengthened by double strips of wood inclosing the edges of the sheets of bark, the whole being bound together by sewing of a specially substantial character. This formed the gunwale of the boat. It was in some respects like the upper edge of a strong basket, which is usually reinforced in a similar way. The boat itself was in reality an open-work basket, sheathed on the outside with sheets of birch bark.

Canoes thus made, though light and buoyant, were quite frail. It was necessary to step very lightly in getting into one of them, for fear of breaking through the bottom, and to sit very still when in, for fear of rolling it over, for the bottom was perfectly round and smooth.

Log Canoes

In some parts of the country, where birch bark could not be procured for sheathing, it was customary to make boats of logs.

It would at first seem difficult to imagine how a party of savages, without any cutting tools, could take down a large tree, hollow it out, and fashion it into a canoe. They accomplished the work by the agency of fire. In the first place, after selecting a suitable tree for the purpose, they would build a fire around its roots, and by constantly bringing more wood they would keep the fire up for many days, until at last the tree was burned so nearly off that by pushing all together against it on one side, by means of poles, or pulling with a cord, they would cause it to lean a little out of the perpendicular, and then its own weight would bring it with a great crash to the ground.

This was the first stage of the process. The next was to burn off the stem of the tree at the right length for the proposed canoe. In burning it off thus the workmen took care to manage the fire in such a way as to give to the end of the proper shape, and at the same time that this process was going on the fire was continued at the other end, in order to burn off the splinters and superfluous wood, and to give that end, too, the proper form for the bow or stern of the canoe, which ever it was to be. To do this well of course required considerable experience and skill on the part of the workmen.

At the same time fires were built along the whole length of the log upon the top, in order to burn off the convex portion, and then small fires were continues along the center line until the whole interior of the log was burned out. It was easy, by means of water, to confine the fire within precise limits, so as at last to have a well-shaped canoe, with sides and bottom far thinner and lighter, and with general form much more graceful and convenient than it would be supposed possible to produce in such a way.

When the burning was completed the whole surface of the boat, inside and out, was scraped smooth by means of tools made of flint, and of other hard stones of that kind which could be broken so as to furnish a sharp edge. The scraping of the surface of the wood with tools of this sort was, of course, a very slow and laborious process, but when completed the result was to produce a very smooth and regular finish. The boat was then painted. the pigments for this purpose were obtained from various substances found in the ground, such as ochres and other similar earths, and they were mixed with oils obtained from animals.

The final result was, in many cases, a canoe of very large size and of quite an elegant appearance.

Of course, a canoe like this is only produced after considerable progress has been made by a tribe in the mechanical arts. At first, it is said, the Indians used the trunks of trees which they found already hollowed by decay, in places where they grew. To prevent the water coming in at the ends in such a case, they used to stop them with masses of clay, which they kneaded in at the bow and stern.

Clearing Land

The Indians had many clearings when the Europeans first came into the country. These clearings were made for the purpose of raising corn, and they were considered of great value — each one remaining in the same family or tribe from generation to generation, for ages. It was very difficult to make these clearings, since the only way of felling trees was by fire. Then besides, when the tree was down the work of getting out the roots was one of great labor. Thus absolutely new clearings were seldom made. The old ones remained, and each generation enlarged them a little when any increase of population required an enlargement, by burning down trees along the margin of them. The method was to dig about the tree so as to expose the roots as much as possible, and then to build a fire around it so as to burn it off. But this was a very slow and toilsome work, for if it was a living tree the wood was green, and after the outside had burned away it was difficult to get the fire in, so as to make it take effect up the heart of the stem. To promote the burning as much as possible they used to pick off the charred portion as fast as the fire formed it, with sharp stones fastened to the end of poles. In this way, and by constantly bringing fresh supplies of fuel, the tree was at length made to fall.

Then to take off the branches and to divide the stem into lengths small enough to enable them to drag them away — all by the action of fire alone — required great additional toil. It is not surprising, under these circumstances, that the work of clearing land proceeded slowly.

Tilling the Land

The work of tilling the land after it was cleared belonged wholly to the women. The men reserved their strength for the immensely more difficult and dangerous duty of hunting and fishing, and of defending the country in case of war.

In planting their fields the women used clamshells for hoes, and sticks sharpened in the fire for picks and shovels. When the crop was ripe the corn was gathered, and it was stored for winter in holes made in the ground for the purpose. The bottom and sides of the holes were protected by a lining of bark, or of wooden poles set up close together all around them. When the hole was filled it was covered over, and not opened again until the corn was required for use.

Preparing the Corn for Food

Instead of mills to grind the corn the Indian women used mortars to pound it. These mortars were stones with hollows in them. For the pestle another stone was a smooth and round surface at the bottom was used. At first such stones were employed for these purposes as were found of nearly the proper form in their natural state; but in process of time the people acquired the art of fashioning them so as to make mortars of very good shape, and of considerable capacity. Many such mortars, with pestles belonging to them, have been dug up in ancient mounds, or found buried just beneath the surface around old and abandoned encampments in the western country.

The women sometimes made cakes of their corn and baked them in the ashes, but, more commonly, they made a sort of porridge of it, or rather soup, for they usually put in a part of some animal, which the husband had brought home from the chase, to enrich and flavor it. The pounded corn and the piece of meat were boiled in the same vessel until they were sufficiently cooked, and then the whole was eaten together.

Mode of Boiling

The mode of boiling this mess was singular enough. They had no vessels which would bear to be exposed directly to the action of fire. They could fashion copper into some very ingenious forms by beating it with smooth stones and grinding it upon rough ones, but they could not make anything like a vessel of it. Nor could they make any pottery that would hold water and stand the fire. But, strange as it may seem, they could fashion a vessel of osiers, coiling them round in a spiral manner, and sewing each coil to the one below it, in such a manner as to make the work water-tight or nearly so. Any small amount of leakage was probably not of much consequence.

The way in which they boiled their soup in these vessels — it is obvious that it would not answer to put one over the fire — was very curious. It was by setting the vessel on the ground by the side of the fire and putting red-hot stones into it. A single red-hot stone would keep the contents boiling longer than one would suppose, and when one became cool another was put in to take its place. Of course, a great deal of soot and ashes went in with the stone, and white men who, in traveling among the Indians, have been invited to partake of a meal so prepared, have not represented the soup as exhibiting a very attractive appearance when it was ready to be served.

Varied Occupations of the Women

From what has been said it will be seen that all the duties of every kind relating to the home of the family and its surroundings devolved upon the woman — it being her province to relieve her husband of every care except that of hunting, of fishing, and of war. When he brought home the animals that he had killed it was her province to take care both of the skin and of the flesh. The skin she stretched upon a frame and scraped the fleshward side of it with a sharp stone, so as thoroughly to cleanse it, and then made various applications to it and subjected it to a particular course of treatment, which took with them the place of tanning. The effect was to make it soft and plaint and to preserve it from future decay.

The flesh, in summer, they preserved by smoking it. They would dig a hole in the ground and make a fire in it. The fire, being at the bottom of the hole, would, of course, not burn freely, but would only smolder away and make a great deal of smoke. Over and around this hole they would hang the pieces of meat, and then build a sort of inclosure, with mats, around them, in order to confine the smoke. The mats formed, in fact, a species of funnel through which all the smoke must pass as it ascended into the air.

The holes for these fires they dug with their sharpened sticks and clam-shell hoes.

Moccasins

It was the duty of the women to make clothing from the skins after they were cured. The clothing consisted of moccasins for the feet, tight leggins for the legs, and a sort of a double apron, with one flap behind and another before, which was worn both by the women and the men. There was also a looser garment for the shoulders when the weather required it.

All these garments were made with great care, and often a vast deal of labor was bestowed upon them. They were adorned with fringes made of hair dyed of various colors, and with feathers of eagles and of other great birds, and porcupine quills, and with embroidery worked in different colored threads.

The moccasins were made of one piece of skin, the center of the piece forming the sole, and the sides being drawn up and gathered over the foot above. Some of them were finished in a very ornamental manner. The fashion of them was very different according to the purpose for which they were intended. Those made for men, which were, of course, destined to endure the wear and tear of long tramps through the woods on hunting expeditions of military campaigns, were made of very stout leather, and sometimes two or three additional thicknesses were put upon the soles.

Those of the women, which were, of course, to be subjected to much gentler usage, were made lighter and of less substantial material; and there was a kind intended to be worn by young women on the occasion of their marriage, for which a skin was prepared by a long and careful process that made it almost as soft as kid. These bridal moccasins were cut in a peculiar fashion, and they were embroidered with hair of different colors, and gaudily ornamented in other ways.

Excursions of the Women

As everything connected with the management of the household devolved upon the woman, it became her duty from time to time to make excursions along the streams or in the woods to procure birch bark to make new rolls, or bull-rushes for mats of other such things. Accordingly, sometimes, when the man had gone away before sunrise, or perhaps even before the dawn, on some distant hunting or fishing excursion, the woman, after breakfast, would prepare for an expedition of her own. In some cases she would take the children, and at others she would leave them at home under the care of an older brother or sister. The number of children was, however, seldom large enough to make this last arrangement desirable, as the Indian families were almost always small. It has been ascertained that the average number of children was only two.

The mother then would usually take her little ones with her and would embark in her canoe. The baby, if there was one, would be tied to a board and lashed to her back; or by means of being thus secured to a board it could be laid down in the bottom of the boat, or placed in an inclined position against one of the thwarts. It seldom or never cried. There were two reasons for this extraordinary quietness — first, the extremely imperturbable and unexcitable character of the Indian temperament, and in the second place, the fact that the poor child found by experience that he never gained anything by crying.

Having taken her place in her boat the Indian woman would paddle her way up or down the stream, or along the shores of a pond, into retired coves or inlets where the rushes grew, and would gather the supply that she required; and then toward evening would paddle home again, so as to be ready to receive her husband on his return.

Sometimes the object of these excursions was to collect and bring home fuel for the fire. In these cases, in order to prevent the sticks of wood from injuring the canoe, she would first lay poles along the bottom of it to protect the framework and the bark covering. For cutting these poles the Indians had stone hatchets, with handles formed of withes bound round the head, like the handles of the hammers already described. Small saplings could be cut off pretty easily with these tools, by first bending them over in such a way as to bring the fibres of the wood near the ground into a state of high tension, when an inconsiderable blow, even with a dull instrument, would cause the stem to snap off at once.

The fuel itself consisted of such dried fragments of wood as could be found already lying in pieces of a convenient size to be removed, or else so far decayed that they could be easily broken into such pieces.

Education of the Children

The children of these families received no education at all until they came to be old enough to learn to set little traps in the woods for small game, or if girls, to begin to help their mothers to make mats or leggins or moccasins. Sometimes they were stationed in the corn-field while the corn was coming up, in order to drive away the crows and other such plunderers with sticks and stones. The boys would usually take to the woods as soon as they were old enough to find their way among the trees. Their fathers would make bows and arrows for them adapted to their strength, and show them how to set traps for squirrels, rabbits, foxes, and other similar game, and great was their exultation and joy when they found anything taken in them.

There is an account of a small boy who set a trap in the woods, and his uncle, who was visiting at the wigwam where the boy lived, went out secretly and put a rabbit in it which he had caught himself in another place. So when the boy went to his trap he found to his great pride and joy that there was a rabbit there. It was the first he had ever caught. He brought it home in triumph and gave it to his mother, and she made a soup of it, and the family with their guest, ate the soup together, leaving the boy to think all the time that it was really the fruit of his hunting that furnished the meal.

Stories for Children

The mothers were accustomed to talk very little with their children. Indeed, the Indians were extremely taciturn on all occasions. They, however, sometimes explained to the children the principles of duty, and told them stories to illustrate and enforce what they taught. Some of these stories are to be found reduced to writing, among other legends and tales which travelers who have visited Indians in their wigwams, or have lived among them, have recorded. The scenes of these stories were laid, of course, always in the woods, and wild animals figured very conspicuously in them. Here is one which will serve as a specimen. It was intended, we must suppose, to teach older children to be faithful, kind and true to the younger ones.

The Child that Turned into a Wolf

Once there was a man who lived with his wife in a lonely place on the borders of a lake. They had two children nearly grown up. The oldest was a boy. The other was a girl. Besides these there was a third child, a boy, who was very young.

The mother was more anxious about this little child than about either of the others, for as she and her husband were considerably advanced in life, she was afraid that they might not live long enough to take care of him until he should grow up and be able to take care of himself.

At last, one day when the father was hunting in the forest he was killed by wild beasts. The mother, with the help of her oldest boy, continued to maintain the family for some time, but at length she fell sick and could do no more. When she found that she was about to die she called her two oldest children to her and charged them to be kind to their little brother after she was gone, and never forsake him. They promised that they would obey. Soon after this the woman died.

For a time the oldest boy remained at home and took care of his sister and brother. But at last he grew tires of hunting and fishing every day to procure food for them, and so he went away and left them.

The girl remained at home for some time after the boy had gone away, but at last she grew tired of taking care of her little brother, and so she went away too.

The child was now left all alone in the wigwam. He staid there a day or two without anything to eat, wondering all the time where his brother and sister had gone. At last, being almost starved, he thought he would go into the woods and see if he could not find what had become of them.

He wandered about all day, and at length toward evening he became so weak that he could go no further, and he sank down upon the ground ready to die. But suddenly he observed near him a she wolf feeding her young ones with the flesh or a rabbit, or some other such animal which she had caught. The little boy crept toward her, and the wolf, seeing how pale and exhausted he looked, gave him some of the meat. This food revived and strengthened him so that he became quite like himself again, and he began to play with the little wolves, and tumble about with them upon the ground.

After this the old wolf, every day when she came home with food for her young ones, gave the boy some of it took, and he continued living with this wild family for some time in peace and plenty.

At length, one day while he was playing with the young wolves upon the shores of the lake, and singing a song, his brother, who was fishing on the lake in his canoe, at some distance from the shore, heard his voice, and he at once recognized it as that of his little brother. His conscience had often reproached him for having forsaken the child, and he was now overjoyed to find that he was still alive. He paddled his canoe toward the shore, and began to call his brother by name.

But from living so long with the wolves, and partaking the same sustenance with them, the child's nature had been gradually undergoing a change, and he was growing like a wild animal. In a word, he was turning into a wolf himself; so when he saw his brother approach, and heard his voice, instead of coming down to the shore to meet him, he gave a wild cry and ran off into the woods with the young wolves that he was with. As he went he sang a song, the burden of which was:

"I am changing into a wolf, and I cannot come;/I am changing into a wolf, and I cannot come."

His brother went away, feeling very sorrowful and sad. He found his sister and told her what he had seen, and during all the rest of their lives they were both rendered very unhappy by the remorse and anguish which they suffered at the thought of having abandoned their little brother in his helplessness, and of having thus been the cause of his turning into a wolf.

MECHANIC ARTS

Native Ingenuity

It is surprising how much ingenuity the Indians displayed in contriving ways for accomplishing their various purposes, without any of the means or facilities which we should have considered essential. They had no iron, and could, of course, have no good cutting tools. All the tools and implements of every kind which were used by the Indians of the eastern part of the country were formed of stone, or wood, or bone, or something of that sort, and although working with such tools was an exceedingly slow and tedious process, still the results that they finally attained were, in some cases, truly wonderful.

Some tribes, especially those that lived in the neighborhood of the great lakes, made certain tools and implements of copper, which metal, it is said, they had some means of hardening, so that it would cut wood tolerably well. But they had no iron. Accordingly, when the Europeans first came to this country, one of the things that principally struck the Indians was their possession of knives. It is said that the name by which the foreigners were designated among some of the tribes was knife men. Columbus found, too, when he first landed in the West India Islands, that the natives would barter almost anything in their possession for a needle.

Manufacture of Weapons

The work upon which most of the skill and ingenuity of the Indians was displayed was the manufacture of instruments to be used in hunting and in war. The bow and arrow was the principle weapon, although they likewise used spears and clubs of various kinds. Their spears and arrows they tipped with heads formed of a stone nearly as hard as flint, which they could shape very exactly by splitting off portions of the mass in a peculiar way, by a process similar to that in which gun-flints are fashioned at the present time. These heads were fastened to the shafts of the spear or of the arrow by means of very slender thongs of hide put on green. These, in shrinking as they dried, would bind the stone to the wood in the firmest manner imaginable.

Great numbers of these arrow-heads and spear-heads have been found in mounds and in old Indian encampments, and are now preserved in museums in all parts of the country.

These weapons were much more efficient than it would be supposed possible that such rude contrivances could be. Of course, in throwing an arrow from a bow everything depends upon the strength of the arm which discharges it. But it is said that some of the western Indians could shoot an arrow swifter than a bullet could be thrown from a gun, and one of them has been known to pass entirely through the body of a buffalo — at least so it is stated on what seems to be very good authority. When De Soto landed in Florida his horse was shot under him, in an attack from the Indians, by an arrow which passed through the covering of the saddle, and entered seven or eight inches into the animal's side.

In one case, too, when a man was killed by one of these arrows, the head of it was found imbedded in the solid part of the bone of his leg, so that it could not be pulled out again.

After all, however, the immense superiority of the European fire-arms became immediately apparent, when the comparison came to be made between the two classes of weapons. Some very amusing accounts are given by the early explorers of the American Continent, of the astonishment of the Indians sometimes manifest when they first witnessed the effects produced by a discharge of musketry. They were not always pleased to find how immensely superior the weapons of the white man were.

Superiority of Fire-Arms

A party of French explorers under the command of a certain officer named Laudonniere, whose adventures will be narrated in full in the third volume of this series, when making an excursion in boats up a certain river in Florida, and landing from time to time to communicate with the Indians, and to trade with them, were received at one time by a chieftain in his village, who in the course of the interview proposed a trail of the muskets of the visitors against the bows and arrows of his warriors. Laudonniere gives an account of the affair in the following language:

"In our discoursing with one another wee entered into speach as touching the exercise of armes. Then the chief caused a corselet to be set on end and prayed me to make a proofe of our Harguebuzes and their bowes. But this proofe, when we had made it, pleased him very little. For as soon as he knew that our Harguebuzes did easily pearce that which all the force of their bowes could not hurt he seemed to be sorie, musing, with himselfe how this thing might be done."

Curious Modes of Making Handles

One of the nicest operations with us, in the practice of the mechanical arts, is that of putting a handle to a tool in such a manner that it shall be firm and strong, and capable of standing the heavy usage to which many tools are subject. The Indians had several ingenious modes of accomplishing this purpose. Sometimes, as has been stated in another place, they made the handle of a withe, which was wound around the took, in a groove hewn in the stone for the purpose. The withe was put on when green, and by this means it could be closely fitted, and then when dry it became perfectly rigid and firm.

Another mode was to make a cleft in a young and growing stem and carefully insert the tool into is in such a manner that the two parts of the stem should closely embrace the groove of the tool, and then leave the whole until the wood should grow over the stone so as to hold it securely. The stem was then cut off and the shaft of it fashioned into the proper form.

Stone-Headed Mace

Some of the tribes had an ingenious way of fastening a round stone to the end of a long handle for the purpose of forming a mace or war-club. They would draw a piece of green hide over the stone, and bring the edges of it down round the handle, and lash it there by means of a thong of the same material wound round and round it, in a close spiral. The result was that the hide, in drying, would shrink and harden, and bind the stone in the firmest possible manner to the handle. By this means a weapon of a very formidable character was produced.

Military Ornaments

The Indians displayed a great deal of skill in making ornaments of various kinds with which to decorate their chiefs when going to war. These ornaments were made of the horns of animals, the feathers of birds, porcupine quills, and of long hair dyed of various brilliant colors. They particularly prized the feathers of eagles for these decorations, on account of the fierce and terrible courage of that bird, which they seemed to imagine imparted an expression of martial prowess to his very plumes.

For the same reason the great warriors chose for their clothing the skins of the fiercest and most formidable beasts of prey. A warrior dressed in full in these habiliments — his spear, his head-dress, his sleeves, and the borders of his garments all adorned with feathers and fringes of hair dyed of the most gaudy colors — presented sometimes a most extraordinary spectacle.

It is quite a remarkable fact that, among all Indian tribes, it was the prevailing fashion for theme to wear the finery. The women were all accustomed to dress in a very plain and unostentatious manner. It is curious to observe, too, that among all the animals inferior to man it is the male usually that monopolizes the gaudy decorations.

Hunting and Fishing

Great was the ingenuity which the Indians displayed in hunting and trapping game and in catching fish, both from the inland waters and from the sea. In hunting they depended mainly on stratagem. Indeed, their weapons were so few and the range attainable by them was so limited, that artifice and wiles became almost necessarily their main resource.

They were very ingenious, too, in contriving traps to set for wild animals. The most common mode of setting a trap was by poising one end of a log of wood, larger or smaller according to the size and strength of the animal to be taken, in such a manner that, on touching a stick to which the bait was attached, the log would fall down and crush the victim beneath it. An Indian would go forth in the morning from his wigwam, and take a great circuit through the forest, setting traps of this kind at different places along the way. He would keep his bow in his hand all the time, with an arrow ready at any moment to be adjusted to the string, and would creep along stealthily as he advanced, looking out in every direction, both on the ground and upon the trees, and noticing every indication, however slight, of any animals being near. He looked carefully for tracks, for marks of browsing upon the trees, for branches bent or broken down, and for every other sign or token which a passing animal might leave.

Solitary Habit of the Indian

In his march through the woods on these expeditions the Indian was always alone. Even if, for any reason, two or more persons were going the same way, they did not walk together, making their observations in common, and beguiling the gloom and solitude of the forest by conversation. That would have diverted their attention and interfered with their work. So in such cases they walked at a distance from each other, each making his own observations and keeping his own watch. It is a general law of nature, as has already been remarked, that wild animals seeking prey are silent and solitary in their habits, prowling about stealthily and avoiding their own kind while watching for their victims. In these hunting excursions the Indian himself was little else than a wild animal seeking his prey, and he was endowed by nature with the qualities that pertain to such a condition.

Summer Hunting

In summer hunting the Indian killed animals for the sake of their flesh, to be used for food, for in the summer, and especially in the latter part of it, all such animals are fat, and their flesh is in the best possible condition to be eaten. If the hunter took more than he needed at this season for his immediate wants, his wife preserved the surplus by smoking or drying it in the manner already explained.

In these summer excursions the Indian often went in his canoe, following the streams or the shores of a lake or pond, and landing here and there in secluded places, to go in among the thickets and set his traps, or examine those set the day before. Generally he was alone in his canoe. If, however, he had a companion, they both preserved the same silence and caution as when on the land. Each would, in his own part of the canoe, ply his paddle, watching the shores of the stream and the trees which overhung the bank, as the boat went on, and looking earnestly into every hidden recess. Thus they would glide on without a word. On such excursions they deemed it necessary that silence, vigilant and constant circumspection, and a readiness that was never off its guard to spring forward in an instant, whenever an emergency might arise requiring sudden action, should be maintained without any intermission; for besides the danger that by inattention they might miss their game, their own personal safety was at stake. A wild beast might at any moment spring upon them from a thicket, or a shower of arrows from a party of human enemies come whistling through the air from some unobserved ambuscade.

All their faculties were thus kept, on these excursions, in a state of close and constant tension, and being engaged as they were, for a great portion of their time, in these pursuits, they acquired the habit of being silent, grave, watchful and cunning, in all their demeanor.

Night Hunting

Among some tribes a practice prevailed of hunting deer in a very singular way, and one in which there must sometimes have been produced a very striking and picturesque effect. The method was by fascinating the deer, as it were, by means of a bright fire made to float down at night on a solitary stream. The fire was built upon the bow of a canoe — a small platform covered with sand having first been made there to serve as a fire-place. Behind the fire a thick screen, made of the branches of evergreen trees, was placed, and behind this screen the hunter was concealed, armed with his bow and arrow, and ready for instantaneous action.

The deer, seeing this bright light upon the water, would come down to the brink and gaze at it, under the influence of a sort of fascination, by which he was spell-bound, as it were, and held motionless on the shore until the boat came near enough for the hunter to transfix him with his arrow.

Snow Shoes

The snow shoe which the hunter used in winter was substantially a flat piece of basket work, of an oval form, which formed a broad extension of the sole of his moccasin, and prevented his foot from sinking beneath the surface of the snow, whether it was the light, powdery drift of a fresh fall that he was walking upon, or the damp, heavy mass into which the beams of the sun transform the old snow of the woods and fields in the spring.

A snow shoe, such as the Indians used, is made as follows: First, a strip of flexible wood is bent into an oval from for the outside frame. Two bars are then carried across from side to side and lashed to their places by thongs of green hide. These bars serve the double purpose of bracing the outer rim and keeping it to its form, and also as points of support for the heel and toes. The interstices of the frame thus made are then filled by stretching a skin over them and sewing it to the outer rim, or by weaving in, over the intervening space, a sort of basket-work of thongs.

When the shoe is to be put on, the toe is slipped under a strap attached to the front bar and is fastened there. The heel is not fastened, but rises from the shoe when the foot is lifted, so that the shoe is raised and moved by the toe alone. Indeed, the heel of the snow shoe is not raised at all in the act of walking. The toe only is lifted, and the heel is dragged along upon the snow till the toe is put down again. Of course, it is only a very inconvenient and shuffling kind of walking that can be performed in this way, but it is much better than sinking at every step two or three feet into the snow.

Adventures in the Woods

Of course the Indians, in their excursions in the forests, were sometimes themselves attacked by wild beast that had been made fierce by hunger or had become excited in other ways. The forests which they traversed were inhabited by bears, wolves, wild cats, and other ferocious beasts of prey, that often, when hungry, would attack men. And even the more gentle and peaceable animals, such as the buffalo and the moose, during certain seasons and in certain states of excitement, sometimes became formidable. The Indian was generally prepared for these encounters, and, notwithstanding the inferiority of his weapons, he almost always came off victorious from them.

A story is related of a young Indian who had been setting traps in the woods and was returning home, when suddenly he saw among the trees a large moose coming toward him with a very threatening air. He had nothing with him but a knife — one probably made of stone. He retreated behind a tree; the moose advanced. He watched his opportunity and fell behind another tree — the moose advancing all the time and tearing up the ground with his hoofs, evidently in a state of great excitement. The Indian contrived, while dodging about from one tree to another, to get out his knife and cut a pole. He also pulled off one of his moccasins and drew out the string which tied it. By means of this string he lashed his knife to the end of his pole, thus forming a rude sort of spear.

All the time while he was making these preparations the moose was hotly pursuing him, and he could only keep out of his way by running from one tree to another, by which means, however, he could only gain a moment's shelter at a time.

When at length the weapon was completed he attacked the moose in his turn, aiming his thrusts at the animals' throat, and still seeking shelter behind a tree after every blow. At length, after a long contest, during which many wounds were given, the moose became exhausted with his frantic exertions and his loss of blood, and he was finally killed

When afterwards the friends of the Indian came with him to the place, to secure the carcass, they found the grass and the underbrush trampled down and covered with blood for a great distance around.

Fishing

The Indians evinced a great deal of ingenuity in their contrivances for fishing. They could make a sort of twine by twisting together the fibers of a certain kind of bark, and with this they could make nets. In setting these nets they used pieces of wood for floats, and stones for sinkers. In the winter they would sometimes set these nets beneath the ice by making a row of holes in the ice along the line where they wised the net to be placed, and then they would contrive by some means to pass the net underneath from one hole to another, till it extended the whole length of the line, and when in this position the stones would carry it down to the bottom.

Sometimes in the summer they used to take fish by shooting them with an arrow while they were swimming in the water, they themselves standing on the bank and watching till they saw the fish come sufficiently near. In such cases a string was attached to the arrow, by means of which the fish could be drawn to the land and the arrow also recovered. Any young reader of this book, who may feel disposed to ascertain practically what degree of difficulty attends this mode of fishing, may easily make the experiment by heating a large fish-hook in the fire, in order to take out the temper, and then carefully straightening it and inserting it into the end of his arrow, and shooting at any fishes which he may see swimming near the shore. Before he succeed in hitting many of them, he will have to learn something about the refraction of light, as affecting the apparent position of objects seen under water, which boys are not all supposed to understand.

It is astonishing to what perfection of workmanship some of the Indians attained in the fabrication of their bows and arrows. The bows were formed of various materials, and sometimes, as, for example, when they were made of substances like horn, they were spliced and strengthened in a very ingenious manner. A western traveler saw one a few years since in the hands of a chief which was worth the price of two horse, and he actually bought two horses, at twenty-five dollars a piece, to give in exchange for the bow. The string was made of the sinews of a deer.

The arrows, too, were very nicely made. There were two kinds, one for hunting and one for war. A good quiver would contain a hundred arrows, and an expert hunter could, if necessary, draw and shoot fifteen or twenty in a minute, running all the time at the top of his speed, either toward or from his enemy or his game.

Sometimes, instead of shooting the fish with arrows, the Indians speared them through the ice. In this latter case they would first make a hole in the ice, and then lie down upon their faces over it, so as to look into the water. They would then cover their heads with a mat or with evergreen boughs, in order to protect their eyes from the glare of the sun, and in this way they could see almost or quite to the bottom. They would then put down through the hole a little fish on the end of a pointed stick for bait. They would hold this stick in the left hand, and with the right they would hold the spear, and when the fish came to the bait, with a sudden and very dexterous thrust of the spear they would impale him.

They had a very ingenious sort of spear which they used on this and on other occasions. it had several prongs, and each prong was armed with a sharp point made of bone or of horn, and dexterously fastened to the wood in such a manner that it could be thrust into the fish, and yet so slightly fastened that when the fish struggled to escape, the point would come off and remain sticking in his flesh. There was a cord attached to the point, which passed up into the hand of the fisherman. Thus, when the fish was pierced and attempted to swim away, the fisherman could control his motions by the line, just as an angler does at the present day, and so finally, when he became exhausted, bring him to the land. This was the nearest approach to our contrivance of a fish-hook which they were able to accomplish. Some of these spear-heads were very nicely made, and were barbed by means of a second point delicately lashed to the principal one at the proper angle. Sometimes these points were made of thorns.

Various Manufactures

The Indians were accustomed to fabricate various other articles of simple construction and use, such as a sort of awl, or rather stiletto, from a thorn, by which, in sewing, they made holes for the thread, in the skin, or the birch bark, or whatever the material might be that they were at work upon. Besides leggins and moccasins, they made a number of other useful articles by means of these needles, such as pouches to told tobacco, and small bags called paint-bags, to contain ochres and other pigments which they used to paint their faces with, and also quivers to contain their arrows. Some of these things were made plain, but others were ornamented with embroidery, fringes of dyed hair, feathers, porcupine quills, and other such things, in a most elaborate manner.

In weaving mats they used a long, slender piece of bone for working in the filling — the rushes forming the warp. This bone served the purpose of a shuttle, and the mats woven by it were very compact and strong. The shuttle had a cleft formed in each end, so that the thread that was used for the filling could be wound upon it.

They manufactured also a great variety of pipes, some of them considerably artistic in form and finish. The material of these pipes was usually some sort of stone soft enough to be worked by such tools as they could command, but often they were made of clay and baked in the fire. When made of stone the bowls were ground out by means of a hard-pointed stick, of the shape of the intended cavity, worked with sand and water.

Painting the Face

The custom of painting the face and other parts of the body seems to have originated in that of oiling the skin, which, it is said, produced a salutary effect in the summer by checking the perspiration in some degree, and defending the person from the attacks of insects. This latter end was the better attained when some foreign substance was mixed with the oil, and in choosing the substance to be applied it was natural that savages should soon learn to fancy something that was ornamental as well as useful. In certain tropical countries, where the natives are in a state of great barbarism, a custom prevails of anointing the body with a wash of thin mud or clay, which, when it is dried and hardened, forms a coat that the proboscis of gnats and midges cannot penetrate. The Indians, with their colored ochres ground in oils which they had obtained from the beavers and the bears, considered themselves doubtless on a far higher level of refinement and civilization than such poor savages as these, daubed with a mere paste of clay.

The Tikkinagon

Although the women were very little in the habit of decorating themselves, but surrendered all fringes and feathers and other such finery to their husbands and sons, they sometimes expended a great deal of time and labor in making and decorating the little cradle, if cradle it may be called, which was prepared for the baby. In the language of some of the tribes it was called a Tikkinagon.

This contrivance, as has already been said, was formed of a board, or of some flat fabric of their own make equivalent to a board. Near the foot of it was a projection like a shelf to support the baby's feet. This projection was often curved so as to come up a little way on each side of the legs, in order to support them laterally. There was a socket made for the head, which was padded with soft moss, and there was a strap which came over the forehead when the baby was put into its place, so as to stay the head and keep it from rolling about. There were other bands which passed across from side to side over the breast and thighs of the baby. The whole was often very elaborately made, and all the bands and borders were ornamented with carvings and embroidery in a very curious manner.

The position of the poor baby, when put into a Tikkinagon, was, of course, fixed and immovable, for his head and limbs were fastened in every part, so that he could not move them at all. In this condition he looked more like an Egyptian mummy that had been three thousand years embalmed, then like a living child just coming forward into being. He bore the confinement, however, with a stoicism characteristic of his race. Whether in his rigid and unyielding couch he was strapped to his mother's back upon a journey, or laid down upon the bottom of a goat, or hung up in a tree, he was silent, patient, motionless, and, to all appearance, totally unconcerned; thus showing that the very low degree of sensibility, both to excitement and to pain, and the emotionless and passive taciturnity which so strongly mark the race, were qualities native and hereditary, not acquired.

The Tikkinagon, however, sometimes contained a slight recognition of the baby's claim to be provided with something to occupy and amuse him, as a strip of elastic wood was not unfrequently attached to the board, with certain little shells and pebbles fastened to the end of it, in such a manner that, when the board was swinging from a tree, the little nursling would have those toys jingling before him.

Fire

The Indians manifested much ingenuity in their mode of obtaining fire. It was very seldom that it was necessary to do this by artificial means, for they were very careful not to allow the fires in their wigwams to go out; and if at any time one went out the others were at hand from which to renew it. Preserving their fires was thus an object of special attention. At certain places where councils were held provision was made, as in the case of the vestal temple in Rome, for keeping up a perpetual fire.

Still it would often happen that hunting parties far away from home, and sometimes the inhabitants of a solitary wigwam, would be without fire, and without any means at hand of obtaining it except by some artificial process. It is well known that all friction produces heat, and that the friction of two dry pieces of wood, if sufficiently violent and long continued, will inflame them, but it is very difficult, without some appropriate machine, to maintain a powerful friction long enough to produce the effect. Very few civilized men can get fire from dry wood by such a process.

The way in which the Indians managed it was this: They would first make a small cavity in a piece of very dry wood of a certain kind — it was only wood of a certain kind that would answer the purpose. They made the cavity by boring into the wood with the point of a sharp stone. Then they would select a long, round stick — which must be also perfectly dry — and from the end of it to a point rudely fitting the cavity which they had bored.

To perform the operation, after the arrangements were thus made, required three men. Setting the stick upright in the hole, one of the men would take hold at the top, and by rolling it to and fro between his two hands would cause the point to turn rapidly this way and that in the cavity. He would bear down also with his hands as he rolled the stick between them, in order to keep the point of the stick in the hole and also to increase the friction. But, in consequence of this bearing down, his hands would gradually descend as he rolled. When he had nearly reached the bottom the second man stood ready to begin at the top by taking the stick between his hands in the same manner. By this means the rotation of the point of the stick in the hole was kept up without any intermission until at length smoke, and soon afterward sparks of fire, would appear.

The third person engaged in the operation stood by all the while watching the process, and holding apiece of punk, or spunk, as it is sometimes called, in his hand, ready to catch the first spark as soon as it should appear. As soon as his punk was on fire he would blow it with his breath, and finally, by means of it, set fire to a little heap of dried leaves and sticks which he had previously collected for the purpose.

Wampum

One of the most curious things connected with Indian ingenuity and art was wampum. Wampum served many important purposes in the domestic and social economy of all the tribes. It was used as a material for ornaments, as money, and also as a means of making records and documents of all kinds.

It consisted of strings of what might be called beads. These beads were made of shells found upon the sea shore, and worn to a proper form by being rubbed on stones of a sandy texture. They were flat and round, about half an inch in diameter, and perhaps an eighth of an inch thick. There was a hole in the center of each by which it could be put upon a string. There was a certain number which formed what was called a string and a number of strings fastened together, side by side, formed a belt.

There were two principal kinds of beads, the white and the purple. The white were made from any shell that would furnish material of that color, and were of much less value than the others, which were made of shells that were more rare.

The strings and belts of different colored beads, variously intermingled, were used a great deal for ornaments, in the form of bracelets, necklaces, and the like. They were also used as money. For a small purchase a string was sufficient, and for a larger one a belt. Sometimes, to adjust the payment exactly to the price agreed upon, one or more strings would be attached to a belt, or additional beads to a string.

After the white men came into the country, and by their dealings with the Indians established, in some sort, the relative value of these beads and English money, six beads of the common sort were reckoned at one penny.

In the treaties made by the early settlers with the Indian tribes, and in various other transactions in which they were mutually concerned, we read of great quantities of wampum being passed from one party to another in making payments. In such cases the amount was reckoned by fathoms, and many hundreds of fathoms were sometimes stipulated for, to be received or paid in important transactions. When the Indians had these large amounts to pay, it sometimes required many months for them to make up the sum, and in such cases they would often pay a portion on account, and ask an extension on the balance due.

Of course, the wampum so paid to the colonists was of no use to them except to pay back to individual Indians again in exchange for baskets, furs, skins, and other articles that were really useful to the settlers.

Wampum Used for Records and Documents

Another very important use to which wampum was applied was for records and accounts, and indeed for documents of all kinds. The people had a way of arranging beads of various kinds. For example, one arrangement denoted a beaver skin, another a certain amount of corn. Another combination would denote a promise to give or to pay, and others still would represent the persons who were parties to the transaction. On the same principle there were symbols to denote days, or weeks, or months, and others representing different numbers. it is obvious that by combining these symbols in a proper manner a rude memorandum might be made of any simple transaction, which, if it could not be perfectly understood without explanation by a third person, was at least a very good memorial for the use of parties to it.

In one respect this mode of executing bonds and promissory notes was superior to ours, inasmuch as in the case of the failure on the part of the promissor to perform his promise, the obligation which he had given was not, as with us, waste paper, but, so far as it went, it was cash in itself, and could be spent as such like any other money.

Treaties and Public Records

Treaties were made in this way, and records kept of all important events and transactions in the history of the tribes; and it is said that at stated periods the great sachems were accustomed to assemble around their council fires and look over the public wampum, to refresh their memories in respect to the meaning of the different strings, and to explain it to the young chieftains, in order that a proper understanding of the facts and transactions recorded by them might be handed down from generation to generation.

It is obvious that without some precaution of this kind the precise significancy of these rude records would soon be lost. And yet it was found that the memory of the to any transaction, when assisted by a memorandum of this kind, was exceedingly tenacious. A story is told of a European who, having received some favor from an Indian, gave him a string of wampum, saying that it was a pledge that he was the Indian's friend, and that if any occasion should ever arise he would serve him to the utmost of his power. Forty year afterward the Indian, being then old, friendless and destitute, came to the gentleman, bringing the wampum with him, and claimed the performance of the promise, offering the wampum at the same time as proof that the promise had been given. The gentleman at once acknowledged the obligation and honorably fulfilled it.

Pictorial Writing

A great number of the Indian tribes had another mode of recording transactions and events besides this contrivance of wampum, and that was by rude drawings representing pictorially the transaction or event which they wished to describe. The material on which these drawings were made was usually birch bark, which makes a very good paper for such a purpose. But sometimes the figures were painted upon the smooth surface of a rock by the wayside, or upon the stem of a tree, the rough outer bark having been first scraped away.

For the purpose of making these records, every considerable hunter had a certain symbol, usually the form of some animal, which stood for his name, and was known to all his acquaintances. There was some sign to show when the figure of the animal was to be understood in this symbolic sense and when it was to be taken literally. All visible objects were represented, of course, in rude drawings, in outline, of the objects themselves. Then there were certain principles of arrangement, and various arbitrary signs, that were well understood among the people, which, in connection with the use of these figures, enabled them to communicate quite a complicated piece of information in a comparatively simple yet intelligible manner. This mode of communicating ideas will be best illustrated by an example.

The engraving is the exact copy of a notice posted up on a pole in the woods by the Indians of a certain company that had encamped there during the night and which was left in order to give information respecting themselves to others who might afterwards visit the spot. It was a company consisting chiefly of Europeans, though there were two Indian chiefs who acted as guides, and it was these two Indians who posted the notice. The European portion of the party consisted of a commander and five persons appointed to various functions under him, such as secretary, surveyor, mineralogist, and the like. These are represented by a row of figures in the center of the picture, reading them from right to left in the order in which such a column would march. The first man is the commander, as is denoted by his sword. The others are represented by appropriate symbols — the secretary with a book, the mineralogist with a hammer, the surveyor with instruments, and so on. These objects which appear small and indistinct in the engraving, which is much reduced, were large enough to be distinct in the original.

That these men were Europeans is denoted by their wearing hats.

Next to them, at the end of the middle line, to the left, are two Indians, shown to be such by their being bare-headed. Beyond is a fire, showing that these persons formed one mess at their encampment.

Above is a line of figures denoting that the party was escorted by eight soldiers armed with muskets, who together formed another mess, as is denoted by their fire. The men and the muskets are represented separately. This was to simplify the work of making the drawing — it being less difficult to draw the guns by themselves than in the hands of the men. On the corner below are delineated the figures of two animals which had been killed the day before for food.

This document, executed upon a large piece of birch bark, was attached by the Indians that made it to a pole which was set in the ground in a slanting direction, the top of the pole pointing out the course which the party making the record had taken in continuing their journey.

It is curious to observe in the work, especially in the mode of drawing, the men, how ingeniously the artists contrived to make their delineations as much as possible by straight lines, and with very few of these in each figure. This was quite necessary, considering the intractable nature of the materials which they had at command, and the very moderate degree of skill which they were able to exercise in using them.

INDIAN LEGENDS AND TALES

Travelers Among the Indians

In every period since the first arrival of Europeans in the country there have been many persons who have taken great pleasure in visiting the Indian tribes, and even in living among them for considerable periods, for the purpose of studying their manners and customs, learning their language, and listening to their legends and tales; and many of these visitors, on their return to the civilized world, have published what they have thus discovered.

The tales and legends which some of these travelers say were related to them from time to time, as they sat on some summer evening in the open air amid a little circle of listeners gathered from an Indian encampment, or assembled in winter around the wigwam fire, are, or at least many of them are, exceedingly curious, and they give us considerable insight into the manners and customs, And still more into the ideals and sentiments which prevailed among the different nations. The following are among some of these legends. The first is an account of the origin of man, as given by a tradition handed down by one of the western tribes:

Origin of Man

In ancient times there was a snail living upon the banks of the Mississippi. He lived there in peace and quietness for some time, until at last a great inundation came and he was in danger of being drowned. He crawled upon a log to save his life, and while he was upon it the log was lifted up by the water and borne away down the stream.

At length it was cast upon a bank and the snail crept off from it to the shore; but instead of landing upon hard ground he found only mud and slime. He crawled along over the soft surface a little way, but presently the sun came up, and shining very hot, it suddenly dried up in the mud, and, as it were, baked the poor snail in.

He struggled for some time to get free, and at last, faint with hunger and exhausted with fatigue, he was about giving up in despair when suddenly he found himself undergoing a strange transformation, and at the same time increasing marvelously in a size. Legs were growing out from him below and a head and arms above. In short, he found himself turning into a man.

The transformation was soon complete, and he stood out upon

the bank changed into a perfect human form, but emaciated and weak, and more hungry than ever. Indeed, he was almost starved. He was naked, too, as well as hungry, and thus his limbs were exposed and defenceless. Though he saw birds flying around him in the air, and land animals moving to and fro, he did not know how to proceed in order to procure food and clothing from them.

At length the Great Spirit appeared to him and called him by name, expressing, at the same time, a feeling of kindness and sympathy for him in his destitute and helpless condition.

The Great Spirit brought him a bow and arrow and showed him how to shoot a deer with it. When the deer was killed he showed him that the flesh was good for food.

When the man had cooked his food and eaten it and thus appeased his hunger, the Great Spirit told him that cold winds and rains would come, and that he must make himself some clothing to protect his limbs from them; and he taught him how to make a garment from the skin of the deer which he had killed.

The Great Spirit also put a string of wampum round his neck, saying to him as he did so, "This is the badge of your authority over all the animals of creation."

The Great Spirit then disappeared.

The man, after this, in rambling on through the country, met the beaver. He commanded the beaver to submit to him, and showed him the necklace of wampum which the Great Spirit had given him as the badge of his authority.

But the beaver, instead of simply complying with this demand, took the man home with him to his lodge. The man was very kindly received by the beaver's wife and children, and he learned from inspection of the lodge in which they lived how to build a house for himself.

Very soon he fell in love with the beaver's daughter and demanded her in marriage. His demand was acceded to, and in due time the marriage was celebrated.

It was a very great wedding. All the birds in the air and all the animals in the woods were invited to it, and great were the festivities and rejoicings. From this union all the races of men were descended.

The narrator of the legend, by way of giving his authority for it to the traveler who recorded it, closed with these words:

There is among the other stories one which seems designed to illustrate the value of a contented and happy disposition.

Old Boreas and Shingebiss

In ancient times there was a man named Shingebiss. He lived in a lodge which he had built for himself on the margin of the water.

When the winter came it was very cold. Shingebiss had four logs of wood, and as the winter was to be four months long, he had just one log for each month, and he was consequently obliged to keep very little fire, so as to burn his logs very slowly, in order to make them last until the spring.

He had nothing for food but the fish which he could catch in the stream. But the stream was frozen over so hard that it was impossible to break through the ice. He, however, looked about and found openings or weak places where the flags and rushes grew, and through these openings he caught his fish. When the fish were caught he dragged them home across the ice, strung together upon a string.

At last old Boreas saw him and said to himself, "This man is as contented and happy in this cold season as if it were June. He seems to despise me. I'll go and pay him a visit, and see what I can do to make him feel my power." The name in the original is the Indian name for the north wind.

So old Boreas blew upon him and made him very cold on the side that was turned away from the fire. So Shingebiss turned first one side and then the other to the fire, but still went on singing his song.

Then old Boreas went out upon the stream and froze up all the openings which the flags and rushes had made.

"Now," said he to himself, when he had done this, "he can get no fishes, and will starve."

But Shingebiss did not despair. He continued his search upon the ice till he found new openings, and by patience and perseverance he broke open those that Boreas had closed up, and so caught more fishes; and when he had caught them he dragged them home to his lodge, over the ice, as happy as ever.

"He must be helped by the Great Spirit," said old Boreas. "I can neither freeze him nor starve him. I will let him alone."

There is a love story, which shows that the instincts and sentiments of woman were the same in those rude states of society as among the most highly civilized nations on the globe. It is as follows:

The Story of Ampata

Ampata was the wife of a brave young warrior. She had two children. She lived for a time with her husband and children in great happiness. Sometimes their home was on the prairie, sometimes they built their wigwam in the forest near the banks of a stream. Ampata used to paddle her canoe up and down the rivers in search of bulrushes for mats, or bark for her wigwam, or fuel for her fire. In summer they lived in open ground, but in the winter they chose a more sheltered position on the margin of a wood, where it opened toward the sun. Thus their lives flowed on a very smoothly and happily.

Ampata's husband gradually increased in influence in his tribe, until finally he came to be a chief. This filled Ampata's heart with pride and she loved her husband more than ever.

But the increased rank and importance to which her husband attained, as Ampata soon discovered, interfered very much with the domestic peace and quietness which they had before enjoyed. He now became a public man. His wigwam was always filled with visitors, and as his consequence in the nation increased, his ambition, instead of being satisfied, became excited more and more. At length, in order to widen and extend his influence, he conceived the idea of taking a second wife, the daughter of a noted chieftain who lived near.

When Ampata heard this she was greatly alarmed. She remonstrated with her husband, but he would not listen to her. It would give him greater influence in the tribe to marry another wife, he said, and marry her he would.

When Ampata heard this she was greatly alarmed. She remonstrated with her husband, but he would not listen to her. It would give him greater influence in the tribe to marry another wife, he said, and marry her he would.

Ampata immediately resolved that she would not stay in the lodge to be thus humiliated by her husband. Accordingly, before he brought his new wife home, she fled, taking her two children with her, and returned to her father's lodge almost broken-hearted.

She remained with her father and with his connections during the winter, but her grief and despondency were not at all relieved by the lapse of time. In the spring, when her farther's party were coming down the Mississippi with the furs which they had taken during the winter, she came with them. She had her two children with her in her canoe. When at length the boats began to draw near the falls of St. Anthony, and turned aside at the commencement of the rapids to go to the land, She did not turn with them, but pressed on into the middle of the stream.

The whirl and turmoil of the water became now so violent that the boat was borne onward with great speed, and the paddle was no longer of any avail. So Ampata rose from her seat, and holding the paddle extended in her arms made her farewell lament in the following terms:

"It was him only that I loved, and I loved him with all my heart. It was for him that I prepared the fresh-killed game, and swept with boughs the hearth before my wigwam fire. It was for him that I dressed and sewed the skin of the deer, and embroidered the moccasins that adorned his feet.

"How I waited in my lodge the live-long day for his return from the chase, and how my heart was filled with joy when I heard his footsteps coming!

"My heart was bound up in him. He was all the world to me. But he has left me for another, and life is now a burden which I cannot bear. Even my children add to my grief. I see in their faces him image, and they bring him continually to my mind.

"I have prayed to the Great Spirit to take back the life that he gave, as I do not desire it any longer, and I am now on the current by means of which he is going to fulfill my prayer. I see the white foam of the water — it is my shroud. I hear the roaring of the fall — it is my funeral song. Farewell."

It was too late for her friends to arrest her course. They saw the canoe enter the foam; they saw it poise itself for a moment on the brink of the cataract, and then it disappeared in the awful abyss below.

The story concludes by saying that sometimes now, the benighted traveler, standing at midnight on the shores of the river, sees by the light of the moonbeams, in the opening of the mist and spray, the form of Ampata's canoe just ready to take the fearful plunge. It appears there for a moment on the brink, and then the mist closing over it shuts it out from view.

This story of the poor, disappointed, and forsaken wife may have been true, precisely as it is here related. The next is of a very different character, being an old tradition of a very decidedly marvelous type. it explains how it happens that the dormouse is so small.

Trap Set for Catching the Sun

In former times, when the animals that lived on the earth were more powerful than men, they killed and devoured all but two persons — a girl and her little brother. These two made their escape, and, flying far away into the forests, they lived there in a secret place, in great fear.

The girl was the oldest of the two, the boy being so small that he was utterly helpless. A big bird might have flown away with him, The girl took all the care of providing food for both, but when she went into the woods to get food or fuel she always took her little brother with her, for he was too small to be left alone.

At last she made him a bow and arrow of a size adapted to his strength, and when she went next into the woods she said to him:

"When I have done chopping in the woods and am ready to go home, I will leave you behind a little while with your bow and arrow, to shoot little snow birds that come to pick up the worms that drop out of the wood that I have been chopping."

So she left him in the woods and went home. He staid and did his best to kill the snow birds, but he did not succeed.

When he came home he looked disappointed and discouraged, but his sister told him that he must not despair.

"You must try again to-morrow," said she. The next day she left him in the woods again, and toward nightfall she heard his little footsteps on the snow, outside the lodge, as he was coming home. When he came in he threw down a snow bird that he had killed, and seemed very much pleased.

His sister cut the bird in two and used it, half one day and half the next, to season the broth or porridge which she made for supper.

After a time the boy killed ten birds, and their skins, sewed together by his sister, made him a little coat.

He was very much pleased with his coat, but one day having lain down in the sun and gone to sleep in a place where the snow had been melted away and the ground was dry, the sun singed his coat and made it shrink, so that when he woke up it was too tight for him.

He was very angry with the sun for this, and he declared he would set a snare for him and catch him, to prevent his doing such mischief any more. he asked his sister to make him a cord.

After several trials she succeeded in making a cord that he though would do, and so he set out one night a little after midnight and went through the woods to a place where the sun rose. He made a slip noose in one end of his cord, and then set it slyly in the trees, in the place where the sun was to come up.

He succeeded very well in his design. The sun, in coming up through the trees, got caught in the noose, and his beams became so entangled in it that he could not rise.

The animals in the forests were all very much frightened when they found that it continued dark that day. They ran to and fro and made great inquiry, and at last they found out what the difficulty was. The sun had been caught in a snare.

At first they did not know what to do. They soon concluded, however, that the only remedy was for them to send some gnawing animals to gnaw off the noose. But none dared to go for fear of being burnt to death by the sun.

At last, however, the animal now called a dormouse, which was then the largest gnawing animal existing, was persuaded to go. He was selected because, being large, he would be better able, they thought, to endure the heat. So he went and gnawed off the noose and set the sun free; but he was so dreadfully burnt in the operation that, when he returned, from being the largest it was found that he had become the smallest animal of all. There was very little left of him.

And that is the reason why the dormouse is now so small.

This story suggests another legend in which the incident of the sun being caught in a trap occurs in a somewhat different form. The story is one which a French Catholic missionary learned from an Indian tribe upon the banks of the St. Lawrence, more than two hundred years ago. In respect to the state of intellectual development to which it is adapted, it stands very nearly on a level with the English nursery tale of Jack and the Beanstalk, which, indeed, in some respects, it closely resembles.

Hunting in Heaven

There was once a man and woman traveling together in the woods, when suddenly they were set upon by wild beasts. The man was seized and devoured by a bear. The woman was also in the same manner eater up by another monstrous animal. But their little child, who was just then born, the wild beasts left untouched.

A woman passing by a short time afterward saw a child lying alone in the woods, and was very much astonished at the sight. She wondered where its parents could be, but on looking all around and seeing nothing of them, she took the child and carried it home to her lodge.

The boy lived, but he did not grow. He increased marvelously in strength, it is true, but not in size; so that, although he remained to all appearance a child, he became strong enough to root up great trees, and to perform other marvelous exploits. His name was an Indian word sounding as much as possible like Jackabeck.

The first thing that he undertook was to seek out and attack the monstrous beasts which had devoured his father and mother. He found them and killed them both, and he identified them as the real devourers of his parents by finding his father's beard in the stomach of one, and his mother's hair in that of the other.

In addition to his great strength he was possessed of a certain mysterious power, through which whatever he blew upon was changed by some sort of magic, just as he wished.

After a while he felt a desire to go to heaven to see what there was there. So he began to climb a tall tree, and when he got to the top of it he blew upon it, and that made it shoot out and grow up higher. He climbed up to the top again and then blew as before, and so on continually. He thus mounted higher and higher, until at last he ascended into heaven.

He found here a delightful country, with green fields and pretty trees and flowers, and ever thing charming. After walking all about the place he returned to the tree and began to descend it, intending to tell the story of what he had seen to his sister — for it seems he now had a sister — and bring her up with him to heaven, in order that they might live there for ever.

As he came down the tree he stopped occasionally by the way to build wigwams in the branches, as places of rest for himself and sister in ascending.

When he had reached the ground and had related to his sister what he had seen, she was at first very unwilling to go with him, being afraid to attempt to climb such a tall tree. But she was at last persuaded to make the attempt, and they set out together.

This sister and a little nephew whom she concluded to take with her in the ascent, and they all three began to climb the tree. The sister and her little nephew went first, and Jackabeck came on after them, in order to catch them if they should chance to fall.

Thus they went on up the tree, and whenever they were tired of climbing they stopped to rest at the wigwams which Jackabeck had made among the branches in coming down.

After they had arrived at the top, in order to prevent any other persons from coming up after them, Jackabeck reached down and broke off the stem of the trees as low as he could.

After admiring the beauties of the country for a time with his sister, and congratulating each other on their safe and happy arrival in it, Jackabeck went off into the woods to set traps, as he had been accustomed to do on the earth below, in hopes to catch some animals.

Very early the next morning he went to visit his traps to see what he had caught. As he drew near one of them he saw in it a great glowing ball of fire. It was so bright and so hot that Jackabeck did not dare to go near it. So he ran back to his sister to inform her of this prodigy.

"Sister," said he, "there is a big fire in one of my traps, so fierce and hot that I do not dare to go near it."

"Ah! Jackabeck," said his sister, "you must have caught the sun. He was wandering about undoubtedly in the night, and has fallen into one of your traps. Go and let him out as quick as you can."

So Jackabeck went back, but he found the sun so hot and dazzling that he could not get near enough to let him out of the trap. He was greatly at a loss what to do, but presently on looking around him he found a little mouse, and he blew upon him and made him so large and strong that he could go the trap and open it in some way so as to let the sun go free.

The story that follows, it is supposed, may have been intended to present to the Indian belles the example of a species of mistake which is often exemplified in tales written for young ladies in civilized life, namely, that of acting in a spirit of proud and disdainful coquetry toward an honest lover, and so, as the proverb expressed it, going further and faring worse. It is as follow:

The Story of Moowis

There lived a certain village an Indian girl who was distinguished for her grace and beauty, and was the admiration of all the young hunter and warriors of the tribe. Indeed, she was quite a belle.

Among her admirers there was a very worthy and much respected young man, who went to visit her one day, with the intention of asking her hand. I will call him Ma-mon, that being a portion of his name. The belle, instead of received kindly Ma-mon's well intended attempts to please her, and giving him a respectful and proper answer, turned away from him in disdain, and dismissed him with a peculiar gesture, which, according to the Indian customs, was expressive of the utmost contempt. The young man went away very deeply wounded.

He was indeed so sensitive, and his mind was so much disturbed by this insult, that he could not recover from the effects of it. He was the more deeply and permanently affected by it from the fact that the insult was put upon him in the presence of others, so that the affair was noised abroad throughout the village, and became the common talk of the young men of the tribe.

At last the sense of shame and vexation so preyed upon him that he lost his health and strength, and almost his reason. He would lie upon his mat in his lodge all day long, silent, dejected, and with his eyes fixed on vacancy. He would take little or no food. No efforts could rouse him from this condition. He felt abashed and dishonored even in the presence of his relatives and best friends, and no persuasions could induce him to rise.

At length the time arrived when the family to which he belonged were to take down the lodge, in order to remove to another station; but still he could not get up. So they took down the lodge from over his head, and left him there lying on his couch in the open air.

It was early in the spring of the year, and the ground was covered with snow, but the snow was hard, as is usual at that season, so that they party could travel upon it, their feet making a crackling noise as they walked along over the frozen surface. The young man remained on his couch until the last sound of the departing footsteps died upon his ear, and then he arose.

The ground that the encampment had occupied was covered with remnants and fragments of all kinds, which had been left there by the families which had occupied it. There were bits of soiled cloth, worn and tattered garments, draggled feathers, and old abandoned ornaments of all sorts, some lying on the frozen ground, and some trampled into the snow.

At the sight of all this finery Ma-mon conceived a plan of revenge.

"She thinks more of the dress than the man," said he to himself, " and I will make her a husband that will please her.'

So he began to collect the old garments together, and after putting them in proper form he filled them with earth and snow, which he pressed firmly in, and thus finally produced the figure of a man. This figure he decorated with old beads, feathers, and other things which he found upon the ground, and which, by some sort of magic, he redeemed from their damaged condition and restored to their pristine beauty. The man, too, when he was finished, was endowed with the power of life, and motion, though his body and limbs still consisted of nothing but frozen mud and snow.

Ma-mon put a bow and a quiver of arrows in the image's hand, and then ordered it to follow him. He gave it the name of moowis.

Ma-mon now went on with moowis to the new encampment of the tribe. When they arrives there Moowis attracted great attention. So well formed a man and one dressed so very elegantly had seldom been seen. No one was more pleased with him than the belle. She fell in love with him at first sight, and invited him to her mother's lodge, where he was received with much honor.

Among other marks of attention they assigned the stranger a place very near the fire. But Moowis was afraid to take this place for fear that he might be melted by the warmth, and so, notwithstanding the urgency of their invitations, he insisted on remaining near the door.

This only increased the bell's admiration for him, as she considered it a proof of his great hardihood and power of endurance; and these are qualities which, next to courage, the Indian damsels most highly prize in their lovers.

But we must not make the story too long. The belle accepted Moowis as her lover, and they were married. Very soon after the ceremony was performed Moowis said that he must go away for a time, for there was a journey that he must take. His bride said that she would go with him. He attempted to discourage her, but she was not willing to be left.

So he set out upon his journey, his bride, according to the Indian custom in the case of man and wife, following him at a little distance. He went on at a very rapid rate. She tried very hard to keep up with him, but she found it extremely difficult to do so. She called to him incessantly to wait for her, but he paid no heed to her cries.

Soon, too, the sun came up and Moowis began to melt away. The feathers and beads and other ornaments began, one after another, to drop off from him to the ground, and, as they fell, they returned to their original soiled and tattered condition. Still the bride pressed on, following her flying husband over rocks and windfalls, and through all sorts of rough and marshy ground. She called incessantly to him and looked for him everywhere, but there was nothing to be seen along the path where he had gone but rags, bones, old worn-our skins, broken beads, soiled feathers, and remnants of torn and tattered garments. The bride wandered on past all these things, calling continually to her husband and crying that she was lost, until at length she became perfectly bewildered and wholly uncertain which way to go. She however continued to wander about in her despair, and is wandering still, singing all the time a mournful song, in which she calls continually to Moowis, saying that she is lost, and begging him to come and save her.

Old Red Head

In ancient times there was a famous chieftain named Old Red Head, who was so violent and lawless in his life and character, and was so great a robber and murderer, that he was feared by the whole country around. he lived on an island in a like, and he had a boat with which he used to communicate with the shore.

He was so much dreaded by the people of the country on account of his great strength and ferocity, that even his name became a bugbear, and a great many designs were formed and plans laid for killing him. But thus far none had succeeded.

Not far from the lake where Old Red Head lived there was a family that consisted of a man and his wife, and a boy about fifteen years old.

One evening, when the man had been out all day hunting, he came home to the lodge, bringing a deer. He was very tired and very hungry. His wife began to prepare the deer for supper, and while she was doing it she asked the boy to go down by a path through the woods to the river and bring some water.

But it was dark and the boy said that he did not like to go. The father, when he heard this, accused his son of cowardice, and said, in a sneering and contemptuous manner:

"I don't think you will ever kill Old Red Head."

This taunt stung the boy to his inmost soul. He said nothing, but he felt very deeply wounded. All that night he lay revolving in his mind what he would do.

The next morning he asked his mother to make him a pair of moccasins from the skin of the deer which his father had killed. While she was doing this he went into the woods and made himself a bow and four arrows.

The next morning after this he rose before sunrise, and putting on his moccasins and taking his bow and arrows in his hands, he went out and shot one of his arrows into the air. It went up very high. He observed which way it inclined as it ascended, and then walked off through the woods in that direction, intending to go to the spot where it would come down.

He traveled on all day long, and at night he came to the arrow. He found that it had fallen upon a deer and killed him. The boy cut off as much of the flesh of the deer as he required, ate his supper from it, and then lay down and went to sleep.

The next morning he rose early and shot another arrow into the air. He followed this arrow, as he had the other, and found this one, too, at night in a deer which it had killed. He made his supper from the flesh of this second deer, and then, being fatigued with his long march, he lay down and went to sleep again.

He did the same the third day and the fourth day. His arrows were then all expended. On the fifth day he wandered about without any food, and not knowing what to do. At last he became exhausted with hunger and fatigue. He sank down upon the ground, and thought that he should die.

While he was thus lying upon the ground in despair, he heard a strange sound approaching him, and raising his eyes he saw a well beaten path leading from the margin of some water to a cabin which was very near him, and which he had not observed before, and up this path a strange looking old woman was coming, thumping her stick upon the ground as she came. She wore a sort of cloak, which was made of the scalps of women, and to the top of her staff a number of birds were fastened by means of strings tied to their feet. These birds fluttered over the old woman's head as she walked along, and continued singing all the time.

The woman went into her cabin and took off her cloak. As she took it off she shook it, and as she did so sounds of loud and continued laughter came from the scalps of which it was made. These sounds continued until she had put the cloak away.

The old woman then came out of the cabin and advanced to the place where the boy was lying. She accosted him kindly, and raising him up, led him into her cabin and gave him some food.

Encouraged by her kindness the boy told her his story. He gave her an account of what had taken place in his father's lodge, of his father's cutting sarcasm, and of his having left home on account of it.

She listened attentively, and when he had finished she told him that he must not take what his father had said to him too much to heart.

"Be of good cheer,' said she. "You shall kill old Red Head, and I will show you how to do it."

So she made the dress of a girl for him, and fashioned him a great many beautiful ornaments. She put the dress upon him and also the ornaments. There were feathers for his hair and bracelets for his arms, and a necklace of beads and a girdle. In the girdle she place a blade of grass of a certain kind, which was pretty broad and stiff, and sharp at the edges.

"Now," said the old woman when the boy was ready, "you look like a beautiful girl.'

So she directed him which way to go, and told him that he must journey on by that way until he came to the shore of Red Head's lake, opposite the island.

"There," said she, "you will find a great many young men, who will fall in love with you, and want to marry you. But you must tell them that you are determined not to marry anybody but Red Head himself, and that if he will not come for you in his canoe, and take you to his island, you will go back again to your home.

When this was made known to Red Head he determined to come to the shore for the girl. So he caused his boat to be brought out. The frame of this boat was made of living rattlesnakes, and they, by some sort of magic, were endowed with the power of knowing when anybody came into the boat with any evil or treacherous designs against their master, and of signifying it by hisses and contortions.

Accordingly, when the pretended girl embarked on board the boat, they began all to hiss, and to write and twist about in the most horrible manner. But Red Head was so captivated with the beauty of his prize that he would not heed their warnings. He went on with the boy to his island.

There, after meeting with various adventures and several narrow escapes from detection which cannot here be detailed, the boy succeeded in dissipating all Red Head's suspicions, if he ever had any, and the marriage ceremony was performed. A great concourse of people came to attend the wedding. Immediately afterward, or as soon as the new married pair were alone, the boy took Old Red Head's head in his lap, as he reclined on the ground by his side, and drawing out the sharp-edged blade of grass from his girdle, he cut it off by a single stroke.

He then made his escape, taking the head with him. He carried it first to the old woman's cabin to show it to her, and then went with it home to his father's — his heart filled with pride and exultation.

He was received with every mark of consideration and honor by his family and tribe, and continued to enjoy great renown as long as he lived as the slayer of Old Red Head.

How Algon Gained His Wife

Algon was a very brave and handsome young hunter. One day when he was roaming over the plains in search of game he suddenly came to a well-worn circular track in the grass, with no path leading to it from any quarter.

This seemed to him a strange sight. How could such a track be made without people to make it? And how could people come to make it without leaving any signs of a path, or even of footsteps, in the grass where they came?

While he was pondering on this mystery he heard a rushing sound in the air, as of a great bird flying, and looking up he saw a large wicker basket descending, with twelve beautiful maidens in it.

He stepped back into the thicket, where he could conceal himself from sight, and remained there watching.

The basket or car containing the twelve girls came gently descending toward the ground, being let down by cords from above. As soon as it reached the ground the girls leaped out, and all immediately went to the ring and began dancing about it in a charming manner.

Algon watched them as they danced, and finally fixed his eyes and his heart upon the youngest of them, who seemed to him to be the most beautiful of them all. He came forth from his thicket intending to seize her, but as soon as the maidens saw him they seemed exceedingly terrified. They all with one accord sprang for the basket, and, climbing into it as nimbly as possible, they were drawn up again into the sky and disappeared.

The next day Algon went again to the place where he had seen the ring, in order to watch for the coming of the girls — expecting to see them descend, as on the preceding day, from the sky.

This time, however, instead of going in his own proper form, he changed himself into an opossum, a very curious and artful animal which hides cunningly among the branches of a tree. In this guise he took his place in a tree near the ring. Before long he saw the basket coming down out of the sky. When it reached the earth the girls descended from it and began to dance again, but before Algon had time to come down from his tree and go toward them the youngest of the girls spied him and gave the alarm, and the whole bevy immediately sprang to their basket, climbed into it as nimbly as they had done before, and went drawn up into the sky again.

The next day Algon determined to go once more, but now he concluded to change into a smaller animal than the opossum, in order the more easily to escape observation. This time he resolved to be a mouse.

So when he reached the place where the ring was formed, he looked about in the thickets near, and presently found a piece of the hollow root of a tree lying upon the ground, with a nest of mice in it. He took up the piece of root, nest, mice and all, and carried it out of the thicket to the ring, and there laid it down upon the grass near the outside of the ring. Then he changed himself into a mouse, and took his place with the others in the nest.

He had not been there long before he saw the basket coming down out of the sky as before. The girls stepped out of it and came toward the ring. One of them saw the fragment of the root upon the ground.

"Ah!" said she, "what is this? This was not here before."

So they all stopped and looked at the root, and then began to pull it to pieces. At this the mice all came out of the nest, and ran about upon the ground, The girls immediately began to kill them. At last they killed all but Algon. He, in order to save himself, turned back into a man.

The girls, when they saw one of the mice expanding and assuming the form of a man, screamed and fled. In the meantime Algon's transformation was complete, and he sprang after them. He succeeded in seizing the youngest, his beloved, and in holding her, notwithstanding her struggles, until the others had reached the basket, and had gone off again into the sky.

Being thus made captive the girl soon concluded to resist Algon's love no longer, but became his wife, and the wedded pair lived for a long time together in peace and happiness.

A great many other narratives of this kind might be given, but these will be sufficient. They are pretty fair specimens of the tales and traditions which are related by parents to children around the wigwam fires, and so handed down from generation to generation.

CONSTITUTION AND CHARACTER OF THE INDIAN MIND

Adaptations Observed in the Forms of Animal Life

In stocking the earth with its living inhabitants the Creator has adapted the form and the physical constitution of the animals of each several species to the character of the locality which they are intended to inhabit, and to the mode of life they are to lead. In other words, every being is endowed with powers and qualities suited to the functions which he is designed to fulfill.

Thus the giraffe, being appointed to feed on the leaves of trees, is provided with long legs and a long neck, in order to enable him to reach his food, and the chamois, having to obtain his sustenance from grass growing in the clefts of the rocks and on steep declivities, has hoofs fitted expressly to facilitate climbing, and muscles to enable him to lift himself up to any shelf among the rocks that he can reach, or to let himself drop down a descent where any animal would be killed. Birds that are to search for their food along the margins of lakes and ponds are furnished with long wading legs and near-seeing eyes; while those appointed to find and devour the bodies of dead animals, wherever they may lie, over a wide extent of country, have eyes endowed with a most astonishing extent of vision, and wings of prodigious strength to sustain them in the longest flights, and to carry them up to the loftiest pinnacles of the mountains.

Mental Adaptations

This adaptation of the powers and faculties of animals to the duties, so to speak, which they are destined to perform in life, applies to their mental qualities, as well as to those which are more purely corporeal. A lamb, being intended to feed on grass and flowers, is gentle in spirit, and is furnished with an instinct which leads him to save himself from danger by running away from his foe. The tiger, on the other hand, is endowed with a degree of courage and of combative ardor so great that we call it ferocity; and this simply because he is to live by seizing and conquering a living and resisting prey. The fox, who is to feed upon timid animals that have wings to fly away from him, is made cunning, that he may be enabled to catch them off their guard. For him simple strength would not be sufficient. So the dog, who is intended to gain his livelihood by the services which he renders to man, is provided with a mental constitution which leads him to attach himself to a human master, and to remain faithful to him in every extremity; while other animals, taken from their native haunts and brought artificially into this relation, are with difficulty retained, and on the first favorable opportunity fly away into their native woods again.

Designs of Divine Providence in Respect to Man

Upon a principle somewhat similar to this the different races of men seem to be endowed with different qualities, each being adapted, both in physical and intellectual constitution, to the place it has to occupy in the history of the species.

For some reason or other which we cannot fully understand, Divine Providence has not seen fit to bring the family of man at once into the full possession of all the attainments and enjoyments of which the species is capable, or to the high social state for which their nature fits them. On the contrary, the system which has been adopted for the human race, unlike that seen in operation in respect to any race of animals not connected with man, is that of an exceedingly slow and gradual development. The different regions of the earth have been stocked with different branches of the human family, strikingly dissimilar to each other in their persons, in their physical powers, and in their mental constitutions — each, however, being exactly adapted to the part which they are respectively called upon to perform in the great drama.

The Great Divisions in the Human Family

Thus the races of Central and Southern Asia are endowed with very peculiar physical and mental powers, differing essentially from those of the prevailing race in Europe, which is called the Caucasian race, and both differing essentially also from those of the African races. The differences which exist would seem to be innate and permanent, so far as we can judge from the results — each particular branch being able apparently to attain only to a certain degree of refinement and civilization, and these remaining unchanged, or almost unchanged, for many centuries. The Chinese, the Malays, and the negroes of Africa appear to have subsisted in substantially their present condition from a very early age, while the Caucasian race has been constantly progressive, having built up in succession a great number of independent empires. The Assyrians, the Persians, the Greeks, the Romans, and, following them, the great European nations of modern times, have entirely outstript in arts, in science, and in civilization all the other races of the globe; although many of these other races have possessed, each in its own region of the earth, equal facilities for advancement, and have held them for the same length of time.

Constitutional Diversities

We must suppose, then, that there is a great and permanent difference in the physical and intellectual constitution of the different races — permanent at least in this respect, that it cannot be changed by an human means in the course of any moderate number of generations. Whether these differences have been produced by external causes, such as climate and modes of life, or by some hidden innate causes more or less connected with these, or whether they have originated in some other way to us wholly inscrutable, is at present entirely unknown. We must, at any rate, accept the difference actually existing as a fact, and conform our reasonings and our actions to it — always acknowledging, however, that the inferiority of any race to ours, if we claim that such inferiority exists, imposes upon us a special obligation to be just toward them, and to protect them in the enjoyment of all their rights, instead of giving us any authority to tyrannize over them or oppress them in any way. We may rightfully recognize and act upon our superiority to them in the social arrangements which we make, but we are bound in doing so to consider them as under our protection, and to guard their rights and provide for their welfare and happiness faithfully, honestly, and with feelings of sincere good will.

Mental and Physical Constitution of the American Aborigines

The American Aborigines have been generally considered by mankind as a stern, taciturn, immovable, unfeeling, and yet shrewd and cunning people. Some travelers, like the celebrated Catlin, among others, who spent a great deal of time among the western tribes, maintain that the degree in which they possess these qualities has been exaggerated. Catlin found the Indians at their own homes, in the villages which they had built on the banks of the Missouri and upon the western prairies, as jovial, as talkative, and as full of life and animation as other men. But the prevailing testimony, especially in respect to those tribes that dwelt on the Atlantic coast at the time of the first settlement of the country, represents them as exceedingly grave and stolid in all their deportment, and possessing very little sensibility of any kind. Their power to endure hunger, cold, and fatigue was surprising. This powers was doubtless, in a great degree, acquired by habit, and must of their apparent insensibility was due to a feeling prevalent among them that it was weak and unmanly to complain. Still there seemed to be something in their physical constitution which gave them a greater power of endurance than belongs to the Caucasian race. They felt cold and hunger, and the pain of wounds, much less, and could consequently endure much more, with the same exercise of fortitude, than other men.

Indeed, we might have been almost certain that this would be so. The same kind and watchful Providence which gives the eagle his astonishing extent of vision, in order that he may have power to survey the vast field over which he is to seek his food, and enables the polar bear to sleep in comfort on a floor of ice where mercury would freeze, would surely not impart a delicate sensibility to the organization of a man who was to live by seeking his food in the winter in a howling forest, with a certainty of often passing days without sustenance, and nights without any covering but bushes and snow.

The Taciturnity of the Indians

The extreme taciturnity of the Indians was one of their most striking characteristics. We shall explain it in different ways according as we suppose, that the Indian was made to fit the circumstances in which he was to be placed, or that he was made like other men, and that the circumstances changed him. On the latter supposition he has learned to be silent, from the fact that silence is so necessary for him while prowling through the woods in search of game, or watching against an ambuscade on the part of an enemy.

But talkativeness is the result of a peculiar mental organization, leading to a lively and rapid flow of ideas, ardent sensibilities, and a quick and ready action of the nerves and muscles are connected with the organs of speech. All this nice mechanism would be out of place, in a great measure, with these children of the forest;; and, indeed, it would be worse than out of place, for it might be, necessarily for aught we know, connected with a greater sensibility to pain, which to the Indian would be a very serious evil.

We might suppose, it is true, that the inward mechanism was

with him, at birth, the same in respect to these faculties as in the Caucasian race, but that, on account of the mode of life which the Indian leads, it remained undeveloped. This is, doubtless, to some extent true. But it would seen that the Indian children manifest from their earliest infancy the same low degree of sensibility, giving them the power of bearing without inconvenience, or at least without pain, what would be intolerable to the children of another race, which characterizes their fathers and mothers. The children seldom cry. They remain patient, strapped upon their board, looking quietly about, and content apparently with existence alone; while a white child of the same age is endowed with powers of observation and with mental instincts and propensities so sensitive and active that it craves the incessant occupation of its faculties, and scarcely ever intermits his restless activity.

Where we find peculiarities of temperament thus showing themselves at the earliest age, and continuing to mark the character and conduct under all circumstances to the end of life, it would seem that we are entitled to conclude that they are innate, and, in the individual at least, are not the result of climate or of education, or of any other outward causes.

Cruelty

The American Indians, like all other savages, were extremely cruel in the treatment of prisoners captured in war. They took great delight in torturing them, and often burnt them alive. Whether any palliation for these enormities can be derived from the fact that such inflictions produced a less exquisite pain in sufferers of their race than they would have done in ours, we will not undertake to say. At any rate, it is known that prisoners subjected to such treatment bore their tortures with most astonishing fortitude. Sometimes, indeed, such suffering was voluntarily incurred, under the impulse of some exalted sentiment of generosity, or other strong emotion.

The Father Dying For His Son

An account is given of an Indian who belonged to a tribe that was involved in some quarrel with a neighboring tribe, and one day when he came home from his hunting he found his wife in a state of extreme anguish and terror from the fact that a party of the enemy had come suddenly upon the wigwam during the absence of the father, and had made a prisoner of the oldest son, and carried him away.

The father immediately bade his wife farewell, and putting himself upon the trail of the hostile party he followed them with the utmost diligence. He knew that the destiny of the poor prisoner was most assuredly to be tortured to death by fire, and he was going to offer himself for this sacrifice, in order to obtain the ransom of his child.

He came up with the party of the enemy just as they were making preparations to enjoy their cruel revenge. He approached them with a signal which was equivalent to a flag of truce in civilized warfare, and offered himself as a substitute for his son. "My poor boy," said he, "is just entering upon life. Do not cut him off so prematurely from the enjoyment of it. He is vigorous and strong, too, and is the hope of his mother, and he will be, for many years, the stay and support of the family. But I am old and infirm. My work will soon be done, and I am of little value to my wife and children. But I am just as good to be burned alive for your revenge as he."

This, or something equivalent to this, the old man said to his savage enemies. They acknowledged the propriety of the proposal, and made the exchange. They unbound the young man and gave him his liberty. The father sent him away, charging him to go home and take care of his mother and of the children, and then gave himself up to be burnt to death by a process protracted as long as possible, while his enemies feasted and danced around the fire.

The Practice of Scalping

The practice which prevailed among all the native tribes of North America of taking off the scalps of enemies slain in battle, and preserving them as trophies of victory, has generally been considered a special token of the barbarous cruelty of the Indian character. The practice, it is true, presents a most shocking image to our imaginations, yet, when we reflect upon it, it does not seem to denote any special and peculiar cruelty. It is barbarous, without doubt, yet still perhaps not specially and peculiarly so.

Origin of the Practice

The practice arose very naturally from the custom that prevails universally among all hunting savages, and indeed among all hunting men, whether savage or civilized, of obtaining from the boy of the animal slain something to be preserved as a trophy of the prowess of the hunter in killing him. A barbarous hunter wears the trophies thus obtained upon his person. A civilized one hangs them up in his hall. That seems to be the chief difference between barbarism and civilization in this respect.

The Indians made their dresses of the skins of animals that they had killed; and the fiercer and more furious the beast that furnished the material, the more distinguished and glorious was the attire.

There were many parts of the bodies of these animals that were used in this way. Skins were made into quivers, moccasins, leggins and robes. Horns were used in head-dresses; bones were worked into beads and ornaments of every kind; and long hair, dyed of various colors, was formed into fringes to decorate the borders of garments. There was a particular species of eagle called the war-eagle, on account of his strength and fierceness, whose feathers were prized above all others for purposes of dress and decoration.

From this practice of taking the skin, the horns, the hair, or the feathers of animals slain in the chase as trophies to be used as articles of dress or ornament, it is but a single step to that of preserving a portion of the long hair of an enemy slain in battle for the same purpose; and when the man was dead there was no special cruelty in taking a portion of the skin with the hair. Not that we are to suppose that the Indians could have any feeling that would lead them to defer taking a scalp till after death from motives of humanity, but only that in ordinary cases they would be compelled to do so. It would, of course, be very seldom that a scalp could be taken from a victim while he was alive.

Customs Connected with the Practice of Scalping

The portion of the skin which was taken from the head in scalping an enemy was quite small, only a few inches in diameter. All that was essential was that it should include the crown of the head — that is, the central point from which the hair separates. The hair itself, however, which grew from the other parts of the head was usually cut off too, especially if it was long, and suitable to be worked into fringes and other such ornaments.

A scalp, when taken from the head, was first stretched in a sort of hoop to keep the skin distended while drying. This hoop was formed upon the end of a long pole by bending the end round into a circle, first cutting away a portion of the wood at the end to make it sufficiently flexible. The scalp was placed in the center of this hoop, and fastened there by strings passing out in every direction to the circumference — the long hair hanging down the pole. The pole served, of course, for a handle by which the trophy could be borne in a conspicuous and triumphant manner.

There were certain ceremonies to be performed with the fresh scalps as soon as the party taking them had reached home, by way of public recognition of them as warlike trophies. These ceremonies consisted of feastings and rejoicings, accompanied with songs and dances — that is, if such wailing and unearthly succession of sounds as they made could be called songs, or their horrid contortions and gesticulation dances. When these ceremonies were completed the scalps were considered as duly consecrated, and were thenceforth preserved with great care in the wigwam, or worn upon the person, as badges of the highest distinction and honor.

Treatment of Women

The Indians have been accused of treating their women as slaves, and there is no doubt that the women were always held by them in a state of very complete and absolute subordination to the men. They were employed all the time in arduous labors, but this was a matter of necessity, for the continual toil of both men and women was in most cases necessary for the maintenance of the family. The woman had the house to put up and take down, the mats and clothing to make, fuel to bring for the fire, and the field to till.

But all this probably made no more than her fair proportion of toil and exposure, when we consider the sufferings and danger and fatigue which fell to the lot of the husband in his hunting and fishing expeditions. The privations which the men sometimes endured in their long tramps through the forests, especially amid the snows and storms and intense cold which reigned in all the northern forests for so large a portion of the year, were indescribably great, especially since the indomitable pride of the hunter often presented his returning home, however urgent his own personal necessities might be, without having first obtained his game. Instances have been known of the Indians wandering in the woods until they have become perfectly exhausted, and of their then lying down and perishing hunger, rather than go home to a starving family, without the means of supplying them with food.

Polygamy

Polygamy prevailed to some extent among the Indian tribes. Of course, since the number of the sexes is everywhere so nearly equal, this practice can never be carried to any very great extent in any human community, even if there were no natural instincts in the heart to war against it. There was no law among the Indians restricting men to a single wife, and prominent personages, such as great warriors and chieftains, often accordingly possessed themselves of more than one. The motive which influenced them, however, in these cases was not, as it would seem, a sensual one. but rather a desire to extend their influence by connecting themselves with powerful families, and to aggrandize themselves in the estimation of the community by enlarging their domestic establishment. The practice, however, being in violation of the natural instincts of man and the essential laws of his constitution, led generally to domestic disquiet and suffering, and sometimes to catastrophes which would have comported well with the strength of the sentiment of jealousy in the heart of the most civilized woman.

Intellectual Superiority of the Caucasian Race

We are surprised sometimes, it is true, at the ingenuity which the Indians exhibited in some of their inventions, and it is, indeed, in some sense wonderful that with materials and implements so imperfect they could manufacture such efficient weapons and carry out such serious contrivances. But, after all, when we come to compare a bark canoe, perfect as it is in its way, with one of the ocean steam-ships of the Caucasian race, or the best made stone-tipped arrow ever shot at a moose or a buffalo, with the double barreled rifled carbines carrying an explosive bullet, with which a French hunter lies in wait for an African lion, we learn the immense distance which separates the powers and attainments of the two races from each other. We must remember, too, that the contrivances which we find Indians now using, and which we think so ingenious, are not the inventions of the individuals that we see using them, not even of the generation now upon the stage. They are the results of the combined ingenuity of a hundred generations! It is somewhat the same, it is true, with our inventions; but with us, not only are the results infinitely greater, but the work is still going on with a steadiness and rapidity of progress almost inconceivable. There is doubtless more real invention exercised, and a greater number of new and ingenious contrivances originated and perfected every single year, in any one of ten thousand machine shops and manufactories now in operation in America, than the Indians can produce as the result of the accumulated efforts of all the generations of their race, from their earliest arrival upon these shores to the present time.

Two Great Means of Civilization

But what ever we may think of the intellectual inferiority of the Indian race, the slowness of their progress in the arts of life was not due wholly to that cause. There are two great essential elements without which civilization can never make any rapid progress, or attain to any great height, in any nation. These two elements are iron, and the art of writing. With the possession of iron to make implements and tools, one man, it is found, can produce the food of ten, thus leaving the other four of the half of the community that we may suppose to be able-bodied, to be employed in other occupations. it is in consequence of this release of so large a portion of the community from the labor of procuring food, through the aid afforded by iron, that arts and inventions arise. Whereas, without iron, it requires five men to produce the food of ten, and the other five consist of the very young, the very old, the sick and the inform. So that, without iron, nearly the whole available strength of the community is required for the production of food, the surplus that remains being barely sufficient to provide, in the simplest possible way, for the demands of nature in respect to shelter and clothing.

Again, with the art of writing the progress made in each separate generation is recorded, and thus the goal attained in one age becomes the starting point in the next. It follows from this art a race that possesses the art of writing may be decisively progressive, but one which is without that art can only be so in a very limited degree. In this latter case the greatest part of what any one genius discovers or learns dies with him, and the next genius that arises must commence the work anew. Thus the nation, even if it is always rising, is always sinking back again to where it was before. Nothing but the art of writing, to provide each generation with the means of recording what it has discovered, will enable it to keep its hold and go on continually ascending.

The Indians accordingly, being without this art, made no advance whatever. If they did not even retrograde, they lived from generation to generation the same.

THE COMING OF
THE EUROPEANS

The Coming of the Europeans

The coming of the Europeans to this country brought new races not only of men, but also of plants and animals, into contact and connection with those previously existing here. The result was that, in the course of two centuries, immense changes were produced in the occupancy of the country, new and higher forms that were introduced from the old world superseding and displacing the inferior and more imperfect ones which before had possession of the new.

Changes in Respect to Animal Life

Some of the more remarkable of these changes are well known. Others equally interesting, in a philosophical point of view, but leading to results less conspicuous, have not attracted so much attention. One very striking case is that of the horse. Certain animals of this species escaped from the Spaniards in Mexico and Peru — very likely a small number at first. They found the region around them producing plenty of grass, and the climate mild and summer-like through the whole year. Of course, they required no care on the part of man, and began soon to multiply with great rapidity; and now, after the lapse of three hundred years, herds of them cover the prairies and plains of the middle and southern regions of America in countless millions, and, of course, other animals, that before occupied the same grounds and fed upon the same herbage, have been displaced by them and have disappeared.

It is somewhat so with the cow. Wild cattle, originally introduced into the country by colonizing companies from Spain, now throng the South American plains in such numbers that they are hunted and slain by hundreds of thousands every year for the sake of the hides. And still the numbers are increasing.

The bovine races of Europe, however, have not been able to spread in a wild state northwardly into the prairies of North America, on account perhaps of the fact that the buffalo, a superior animal of the same kind — superior in respect to strength and ability to maintain his ground — has possession already. Nor were they or the horses able, unaided by man, to occupy the northern regions on the Atlantic; for although these regions were well adapted to produce their peculiar food, the winters were too long and cold for such animals to live through them without artificial aid. With this aid, however, they can do it, and thus, under the fostering charge of man, the green meadows and hill-sides, extending over many thousands of square miles between the lakes and the sea, have been covered with flocks of sheep and herds of horses and cows, while the bear and the moose that formerly had possession of them have passed away. A few lingering specimens only remain to roam in solitude within the narrow limits left to them, and to wonder where their companions can have gone.

Changes in Respect to Plants

Changes corresponding to these have taken place on a vast scale in the vegetable kingdom. Multitudes of plants that were introduced into America by the European colonists, either accidentally or by design, have since that time become very widely extended here, and have extirpated or displaced, to a corresponding degree, the original occupants of the soil. These changes have taken place sometimes with and sometimes without the aid of man. One of the most striking examples of the former class is that of the grasses and the cereal grains, such as wheat and rye, which now cover millions and millions of acres through all the central regions of the continent, where formerly brakes and bull-rushes and wild woodflowers, barren and useless, had complete possession.

It is well that this should be so. Such changes are in fulfillment of the beneficent designs formed by the author of nature for the gradual improvement of the condition of the earth, and the advancement of it, in respect to its occupants, from lower to higher and nobler forms of life.

Changes in the Races of Men

A change exactly analogous to these has taken place in respect to man. The aboriginal inhabitants of the country were of races formed with constitutions, both physical and mental, adapting them to obtain their livelihood by fishing and the chase — modes of life by means of which North America might sustain perhaps twenty or thirty millions of inhabitants. The Caucasian race, which was introduced from Europe, is endowed with constitutions adapting them to gain their livelihood by agriculture, commerce, and the manufacturing arts, a mode of life by which the same territory is capable of supporting many hundred millions — we know not how many. Under these circumstances it was an inevitable, and as much in fulfillment of the designs of divine Providence, that the old races should be supplanted by the new, as that the horse and the cow should displace the alligator and the elk, and brakes and bulrushes yield their native ground to corn.

And such has been the fact. It has been estimated that at the time America was discovered the number of Indians dwelling within the limits of the United States was about sixteen millions. Of the descendants of these sixteen millions only about two millions now remain.

The Displacement of One Race By Another Not Necessarily Attended With Suffering

Nor are we to suppose that such a change as this, by which a lower race is supplanted by a higher one, necessarily implies any violence or wrong on the part of the former against the latter, or any special suffering. It is the race and not the individuals that the extirpating process acts upon. That is to say, the effect is produced, not by the destruction of individuals already existing, but by a diminution in the numbers born to take the places of those ceasing to exist by natural causes. If the various aboriginal races had always been, and still continued to be, treated with the strictest justice and the most sincere and cordial good will, they would have none the less surely fulfilled the universal destiny of the lower to give way before the higher forms, in the great onward march of organization and life; but the change would have come slowly, quietly, and without suffering. Indeed, the very beings subject to it, with the exception of a few far-seeing minds that might discover it by a special and laborious study of the past and of the future, would have been unconscious that it was going on.

Difficulties That Opposed the Amalgamation of the Two Races

It might at first be supposed that when a superior and an inferior race were brought thus together upon the same territory, a process of amalgamation would have set in, by which, in the end, they would gradually be melted into one; but there are very deep-seated causes operating in all such cases to prevent such a union. In the first place, the mental and physical constitution of the Indian fits him specially for wandering as a hunter through the woods, and gaining his subsistence by the chase, and for no other mode of life. These qualities are innate and permanent. At least they are beyond the reach of any means of change that can be brought into operation in the course of any moderate number of generations. The whole history of the Indian tribes and of the almost fruitless attempts which have been made to civilize them, and induce them to live like white men, proves this quite conclusively. Missions were established among the Indians of New England for the purpose of instructing them in the arts of European life and in the truths of Christianity, and though for a time very remarkable results were produced, no radical or lasting change was usually effected. As soon as the external support to this new state of things, and in a certain sense unnatural, was withdrawn, everything slowly but irresistibly sank back into its former condition, and the hereditary instincts and propensities of the race returned in all their pristine vigor.

In the same manner the experiment has several times been made of educating Indian Young men in the New England colleges, but the pupils thus taught have, almost without exception, when their prescribed course was finished, and they were left at liberty, as they arrived at manhood, to follow the impulses and instincts of their own hearts, very soon turned away from the arts and refinements of life to which they had thus been ushered, and have gone back into the woods, and relapsed hopelessly into their former condition.

Fixedness of the Indian Tastes and Habits

There are remnants of many of the ancient tribes existing at the present day in various parts of our country, but they live by themselves, a marked and separate race, with nothing changed except the external circumstances by which they are surrounded. They live in huts still, as their ancestors did three hundred years ago. it is only the covering that is changed — the birch bark, which has failed, being replaced with canvass, or with slabs obtained from the white men. They sit upon the ground around their wigwam fire, just as of old, and are occupied in the same species of employment, only that they make baskets instead of canoes, and bows and arrows to sell as toys, or to be used by children in shooting at coppers for a prize, instead of for the service of hunters in the chase. Even their garments retain in a great measure the forms of the old national costume, though made now of blankets and calico, instead of the skins of beasts, and adorned with glass beads instead of wampum. they come with the wares which they make to sell into the white man's kitchen, where they are kindly entertained, and where they have every opportunity to observe the conveniences and the comforts which civilization affords, but no kindling desire is awakened in their minds to imitate or share them. Silent, patient, impassible, they witness the advance of the mighty wave which sweeps on so irresistibly over and around them, apparently without any regret for the past, or any emotion, either of hope or fear, in respect to the future. And thus in the heart of a country changing and advancing more rapidly than any other, they alone remain, from generation to generation, wholly unchanged.

There are descendants from Indians residing in certain portions of the Southern States that have adopted a settled mode of life, and have attained to a considerable degree of refinement and civilizations, but in general, even among these, the degree in which they manifest the capacities of the Caucasian race corresponds very nearly to the proportion of Caucasian blood that flows in their veins.

Present Condition of the Western Tribes

In the interior and western portions of the continent are vast tracts of land which remain almost entirely in possession of Indians; and although the United States government exercises a general jurisdiction over the whole country, still there are extended territories reserved for the exclusive occupancy of the native tribes. Within these reservations the tribes live in their own way, pursuing such modes of life and maintaining such systems of government as they themselves choose. This state of things has continued for more than a century, without any essential change taking place in the Indian habits or character. A very considerable trade has sprung up, it is true, between the natives and the whites, by which, in exchange for skins and furs which they obtain by trapping and the chase, the former procure a great many commodities that are produced by the arts and manufactures of civilized life. But the introduction of these commodities among them does not have the effect of changing their habits or modes of life in any appreciable degree, but rather, by facilitating the supply of their wants and the satisfaction of their desires, to fix and establish these habits more firmly than ever. They obtain from white men horses and guns and blankets, and gaudy trappings and decorations of all kinds. But they use all these things only as means to enable them the better to act their parts as huntsmen and warriors.

The Mandan Lodges

Some of the western tribes avail themselves of their commerce with the whites to procure the means of adding very materially to their domestic comfort, while still not essentially changing the system of life handed down to them from their forefathers. They built lodges of great size, sometimes fifty feet in diameter. The sides are formed, for four or five feet above the ground, of a bank of earth. Above this the walls are continued upward by a row of very stout poles or stems of trees, which are set close together on the top of the bank and meet in the center above. The roof is thatched with willow boughs and then plastered over with clay, so as to make it perfectly water-proof. In the center of the interior is a fire-place, which consists simply of a shallow depression in the ground. This fire-place can, of course, be approached on every side, and it is for the use in common of all the families that inhabit the lodge.

The space at the circumference of the lodge, extending along the wall, is divided into separate compartments, like the cabins of a ship, for the several families. Sometimes very rich and showy curtains are used to separate these compartments from each other, and the posts which are set up to divide them are hung with arms and armor, and also with scalps, antlers and other trophies.

Each family has a bedstead within its compartment. A buffalo skin stretched over it forms both sacking and bed. Another buffalo skin serves the combined purpose of sheets, blankets and counterpane; while a third, properly folded, fulfills the function of both bolster and pillows.

Some of these Indians carry their luxury, in the matter of dress and decoration, very far. An American traveler once gave fifty dollars for the head-dress of a western Indian, which he wished to purchase as a specimen of Indian art, to add to his museum.

Different Causes for the Aversion of the Indians to Live Like the Whites

Great surprise has often been expressed at the total disinclination always manifested by Indians to imitate the modes of living adopted by the whites, after having once had an opportunity to observe the infinite superiority of them. And although the principal cause may be that they are endowed by the Creator with a mental and physical constitution that adapts them to a different course of life, there are other causes that have been combined with this in producing the effect. Among them one was the repulsion of race — a fixed principle of nature that manifests itself universally throughout all the realms of animal life, and has been ordained, as we shall presently see, for wise and beneficent ends, which prevented them from being cordially received into the same social and domestic system with the whites, and treated by them in it as friends and brothers. A great many curious anecdotes are related in books of Indian history illustrating the position which the poor Indian occupied among the whites, and the feelings with which he entertained the idea of living with them and becoming one among them.

The Kennebec Indian and His Child

Nothing can illustrate in a more touching manner the influence of this feeling than the story of the Kennebec Indian and his dead child. The tribe to which this poor man belonged lived on the banks of the Kennebec, in Maine, and when the State passed into the occupancy of white men, it became nearly or quite extinct. One man of the tribe who still remained, so recommended himself by his good behavior, and by his evident desire to adopt the habits of civilized life, that he received a grant of land from the State, in a certain township, and he settled upon this land with his wife and child, while the other farms in the neighborhood were settled by whites.

The Indian was treated fairly enough by his neighbors in their ordinary dealings with him, but still he was an Indian in their view, and they felt no cordial sympathy with him or his family. They did not admit him to any intimate relations with them, or regard him with the kind and friendly feeling which they entertained for each other.

At length his child fell sick and died. The neighbors did not come to see the family in their distress, and the poor Indian buried his child alone.

Not long afterward he went to some of his neighbors, and said to them in his broken language as follows:

"When white man's child dies, Indian man be sorry. He help bury him. When my child die, no one speak to me. I make his grave alone. I can't no live here any longer."

He gave up his farm, dug up the body of his child, and carried it away with him, two hundred miles through the woods, to Canada, and joined a tribe of Indians living there, to share with them, for the rest of his days, the hardships and privations of barbarism.

The Feeling of Repulsion That Exists Between the Different Races of Man Not Necessarily a Prejudice

That peculiar feeling of repulsion which is seen universally in operation between the different races of men, and makes them mutually disinclined to live together in intimate domestic and social relations, is not, as is sometimes supposed, necessarily a prejudice. It results, as has already been intimated, from a wise and beneficent law of nature — one in universal operation throughout the whole animal world — the object of which is to preserve the distinction of species, and to maintain the purity, and secure the advancement, of the higher and nobler races of men. It is an instinctive principle implanted in the nature of every living being which draws him from those that are unlike himself in their physical conformation, and toward those that resemble him. In species that are entirely distinct from each other the aversion to domestic union is unconquerable. In the case of varieties, like those seen in the different races of men, the repulsive instinct by means of which nature intends to keep them separate from each other, in respect to the propagation of their kind, is less strong, but it is none the less real, and the design with which it has been implanted is beneficent in the highest degree. Thus the amalgamation of the Indian race with the Caucasian race coming to the new world from Europe, would have been against nature, and the instinctive principle, both in the heart of the Indian and of the white man, which leads each to love, and to seek domestic and social union with, those of their own race, and to avoid such union with those of the other, was one wisely implanted in the heart by the great author of nature, and one which both races were accordingly bound to obey.

The Universal Brotherhood of Man

These views, which it would seem impossible to gainsay, do not at all conflict with the sublime doctrine which the Christian religion teaches us, of the universal brotherhood of man, and the obligation which rests upon us all to regard every human being with sentiments of cordial and honest good will. They do not in the least excuse the acts of injustice and cruelty which have been perpetrated so extensively upon the Indian tribes during the last two hundred years, in consequence of which the gradual displacement of the old race by the new, which might have proceeded quietly, peacefully, and without individual suffering, has been hurried onward with so much violence and wrong. Let us hope, however, that the period of this injustice is now over, and that the ancient race, though its days are numbered and are fast passing away, may be cheered in its decline by the kind and friendly regards of those that are to succeed to its heritage, and thus be permitted to spend the remainder of its old age in happiness and peace.

THE END

i

www.ingramcontent.com/pod-product-compliance
Lightning Source LLC
Chambersburg PA
CBHW032125090426
42743CB00007B/477